"I have been blessed mega-tons [...] with teens for over thirty years a [...] more pertinent in the life of a teenage boy than his relationship with his father. I believe an all-knowing God planned it this way and calls Himself our heavenly Father to give us a target for which to aim. I know of no other father/son team that is better equipped than Josh and Jim Weidmann to take God's Word and provide a biblical road map to get us there...knowing that every road we travel must lead to the cross!

JOE WHITE
PRESIDENT, KANAKUK KAMPS

"Dads matter. How much thought and effort we intentionally invest in our strategic role as fathers will be reflected in the lives of our sons and daughters. YOU are what your child needs. I like what Josh wrote: 'Your teens love you and want you in their lives.' In this warm and personal book, Josh shows us dads how to listen and connect with our kids. I have known Josh for years. I know of his journey, and now you will too."

TIMOTHY SMITH
AUTHOR, SPEAKER, FAMILY COACH, AND PRESIDENT,
LIFE SKILLS FOR AMERICAN FAMILIES

"Relationship! Relationship! Relationship! Dads connecting with their kids leads to kids connecting with their heavenly Father. When those relationships pulsate with life, then our children, families, churches, and our culture will do a 180-degree turn. And not be a minute too soon. My friends, Jim and

Josh, have demonstrated that father/son connection with God and each other. The lessons they learned in their relationship make getting this book into the hands of every dad a must!"

BARRY ST. CLAIR
PRESIDENT AND FOUNDER OF REACH OUT YOUTH SOLUTIONS

"For several decades, working directly with and indirectly for teenagers, I've become increasingly convinced that the role a father plays in the lives of his children is absolutely pivotal. But by stating the case through the eyes of teenagers (and Josh himself—not too far out of the teen years), the message comes across more powerfully. What would teenagers tell their dads if they felt they'd really listen? Before reading this book I thought, *Isn't it nice that dads who really botch up this fatherhood thing now have something to help them?* But when I was just a few pages into it, I realized that this book is for all fathers—no matter how good or how bad they're doing in this all-important job of raising godly sons and daughters. Personally, despite being a very hands-on father, I came away determined to do an even better job at raising my own teenagers."

BOB WALISZEWSKI
TEEN, MEDIA, AND YOUTH CULTURE SPECIALIST

"At last, a book from a savvy, articulate youth about the longings and aspirations that teenagers have for a deepening relationship with their dads. I can't think of anyone better to write this than Josh Weidmann and his dad, Jim. They have done us all a great favor!"

DR. JOSEPH M. STOWELL
FORMER PRESIDENT, MOODY BIBLE INSTITUTE
TEACHING PASTOR, HARVEST BIBLE CHAPEL

DaD, IF YOU ONLY KNeW...

JOSH WEIDMANN
WITH JIM WEIDMANN

Multnomah® Publishers *Sisters, Oregon*

DAD, IF YOU ONLY KNEW…
published by Multnomah Publishers, Inc.

© 2005 by Josh Weidmann and James Weidmann
International Standard Book Number: 1-59052-486-1

Cover design by Studiogearbox.com
Cover image by Nick Daly/Getty Images

Scripture quotations are from:
The Holy Bible, New International Version
© 1973, 1984 by International Bible Society,
used by permission of Zondervan Publishing House

Multnomah is a trademark of Multnomah Publishers, Inc.,
and is registered in the U.S. Patent and Trademark Office.
The colophon is a trademark of Multnomah Publishers, Inc.

Printed in the United States of America

For information:
MULTNOMAH PUBLISHERS, INC.
601 N. LARCH ST.
SISTERS, OREGON 97759

Library of Congress Cataloging-in-Publication Data

Weidmann, Josh.
    Dad, if you only knew : eight things teens want to tell their
dads (but don't) / by Josh Weidmann, with Jim Weidmann.
        p. cm.
    ISBN 1-59052-486-1
    1. Father and child. 2. Parent and teenager.   I. Weidmann,
Jim. II. Title.
    BV4529.17.W45 2005
    248.8'421—dc22

                                                                2005008710

05 06 07 08 09 10—10 9 8 7 6 5 4 3 2 1 0

Dad, I dedicate this book to you. From my beginning days you have encouraged me in the way I should go—helping me to know Christ and Him crucified, keeping God's Word on the forefront of my mind, and teaching me the eternal power of prayer. You are my dad, my coach, my hero, and my friend. Thank you for being a mighty man of God and molding me to be the same.

Mom, this book is for you, too. Thank you for helping Dad to be the father he is, for being our family's steady heartbeat of Christ's love, and for giving my passion an aim.

I love you Dad and Mom.

—*Josh Weidmann*

First, I want to dedicate this book to my father, Larry Weidmann. One of the most significant impacts on my life has been my dad. By making his children a priority in his life, he was able to model what godly fatherhood is really all about. This book is a tribute to the legacy he has passed. Second, I want to dedicate this to my loving wife. Her unconditional love and nurturing spirit for our children have helped instill their strong sense of worth and spiritual understanding. I thank God for how she completes me. Third, I want to dedicate this to Joshua. His passion for God is a blessing to my soul.

—Jim Weidmann

contents

FOREWORD

BY JOSH MCDOWELL

ABOUT THE FIRST favor Josh Weidmann ever did for me was to turn me down.

It was right after the Columbine High School shootings in 1999. Josh was already neck-deep in a Christian student response to the tragedy, and even though I hadn't met him yet, I called to offer to come speak.

Josh said thanks, but no. The students didn't really want adults talking to them, he said. At least not yet. It was students who had died at the hands of their peers. It was the blood of teenagers—their friends—spilled in school hallways. The only ones they were opening up to so far, Josh told me, were other teens.

Right there I got a full dose of Josh's special passion. He has a heart to reach his generation for Christ, but not without listening carefully first. That's what he does as well as any young man I've met. Wherever he speaks across the country—youth rallies, conferences, high school assemblies, music festivals, concerts—Josh shares the hope of the gospel for our times. He shares himself. And when he's done, teens line up to share their lives with *him*. What do they say? Things they wouldn't think of saying to *any* adult— father, teacher, pastor, you name it.

This book, *Dad, If You Only Knew*, is Josh's careful, passionate, and authentic report back to dads of what he's hearing from our kids. In these pages, you'll hear the truth. You'll hear the heart cry of a generation in crisis. And you'll understand right away where you can start to make a dynamic impact as their father.

I don't need to alarm you by quoting statistics that indicate what our teens are up against these days. They face unprecedented pressures and dangers. They're getting mowed down, chewed up, and spit out by the big, bad world. That, we know.

But do we really know what they're needing, asking for, *pleading* for from their parents? Have we listened—really? Do we know what they need *most* from a dad?

My friend, we can't afford not to listen and respond.

Adding special impact to this report to dads is the seasoned advice of Jim Weidmann, Josh's own dad, who is well known for his Heritage Builders seminars for parents, and his work with Shirley Dobson as co-chair of the National Day of Prayer. You'll find his perspective helpful, practical, and seasoned in Scripture. And as you'll find out, the relationship between Dad and Son Weidmann is genuinely respectful and affectionate—reality-tested enough from Josh's teen years to give them both plenty of great stories!

Since our first meeting, I've been privileged to share the stage with Josh at the one-year anniversary of the Columbine shooting, on Moody Bible Institute's *Open Line Radio*, in front of over sixty thousand youth at the "Acquire the Fire" event held at the Detroit Silver Dome, and at other youth events around the country. More importantly I have had the chance to spend time with Josh one-on-one over coffee or a meal. My conclusion: he's the real deal.

That's why I believe the Lord can use the Weidmanns' book to give Christian dads the tools they need to succeed, and the motivation to do so with all their hearts. I highly recommend it.

Josh McDowell

P.S. Actually, Josh didn't turn me down completely. He gave me seven minutes. Seven times sixty seconds. (Then he whisked me off to a side room where I spent time with area youth pastors.) You gotta love a kid like that!

DaD, IF YOU ONLY KNEW...

PREFACE

DaD, I WaNT to show you something.

It's a line of teens waiting to talk. These kids look pretty much like any teen from anywhere in the country. They've been lining up like this in front of me night after night across North America for the past six years. The line forms every time I finish speaking at youth rallies, school assemblies, camps, and conferences. Trust me, they're not here because I'm so special, and it sure isn't because I have all the answers. The kids just want to talk. Because I've come to challenge them to know and follow Jesus Christ, they know I care. And because I—like a lot of kids in my Colorado hometown—experienced the pain of the Columbine High School shootings firsthand, they know that I can relate to the fears of their generation. So they line up.

To talk about what? Well, the stuff they're doing and feeling and thinking about—the stuff they think no one else could ever dream up. Words tumble out. Sometimes the teens speak in whispers, sometimes they yell or sob. As they talk, I see one fact emerging over and over:

What they're sharing with me, they really wish they could tell you. Their dad.

Sure, it can be hard for a teen to talk to Dad. And often it's not Dad's fault at all. In fact, right now your teens may act or talk like they don't need you at all. Do any of the following describe your recent relationship with your teen?

- Your teen hasn't initiated a conversation with you for months.
- Your teen is embarrassed to be seen with you in public.
- Your teen thinks your taste in music, clothes, and friends is totally off.
- Your teen makes a point of letting you know how much she doesn't need your opinions, advice, time, questions, or maybe (on a really hostile day) even your money.

Take heart, dads. I hear it all the time: If a teen could say anything to you, he'd say, *Dad, I need you.*

Really.

If saying that—*Dad, I need you*—was cool, I think teens would say it all the time. They'd whisper it to you when they got up. They'd text message it to you on their cell phones. They'd shout it from the highest mountains...*Dad! I need you!*

But, well, I guess it's not cool. For whatever reason, most teens are reluctant or embarrassed to talk to you—their own father! Maybe they fear that you'll laugh at them or blow them off.

That's why I wrote this book. I'm a messenger, not an expert. But I love this generation of young people, and I feel called by God's grace to do my part. The lines of teens have convinced me—if we are going to call youth to a saving relationship with their heavenly Father, it helps for them to first have a vibrant relationship with their earthly dad.

My prayer is that the rest of the book you're holding will help you hear what your kids are really saying and respond with your whole heart.

—*Josh*

INTRODUCTION

YOUR TEENS ARE TALKING

NOT TOO LONG AGO I was speaking at a high school in the South. Right in the middle of my talk in the school's old theater auditorium, I heard a garbled yell from the balcony. It was a girl's voice and sounded something like: *"THEYWON'T DOIT!"*

I didn't understand her, so in front of everyone I stopped and asked her what she said. She ducked down and ignored my question, and not knowing what else to do, I decided to keep going with the rest of my speech. Afterward, the principal of the school pulled me aside and apologized for the girl's actions.

"She has a really bad home life," he said. "I don't think she's got many friends here. Her teachers tell me she has a tough time in class…" Mid-sentence, his eyes looked away. I could tell by his look that someone was now standing behind me. I turned around to find *that* girl. She opened her mouth without saying anything, then darted off toward the bathroom. I called her back. The principal offered his office. Before we had even sat down, she began to cry.

"Nobody loves me," she said between sobs. I was floored by how quickly she got to the core issue.

"What do you mean nobody loves you?" I asked. "Surely somebody loves you."

"My dad hates me," she said. "He's hardly in my life at all. He doesn't even acknowledge me when we're in the same room. My dad tells me straight to my face that I'm the greatest mess-up of his life."

The girl pulled up her sleeves to show me long red and black marks on her arms. The night before she had cut along the veins of her arms and jabbed herself with a hot metal rod. She was not kidding. I found it hard to keep breathing. She needed more help than I could provide in a short space of time, but I wanted to clarify something.

"What did you yell from the balcony?" I asked. Her shout had come right at the point when I was telling the student body to reach out to kids who aren't accepted.

"I'm one of those kids you were talking about," she whispered. "I'm one of the ones nobody accepts. I yelled, 'They won't do it!,' because I know they won't reach out. *No one has ever reached for me.*"

How I wish I could say this girl's story was uncommon.

About a month later I was speaking at a weekend youth conference. One night a junior high–aged boy told me about how his dad repeatedly told him he was just one big mistake. The boy lifted the front of his shirt to show me his chest. All across his skin were red streaks. I had never seen anything like it before.

"My dad told me I was just a huge mistake that just needed to be wiped away," he said. "So I took a pencil eraser and tried to erase myself."

> **my dad told me I was just a huge MISTAKE that just needed to be WIPED away**

This was a new one for me. I prayed that God would give me the right words to say next.

"Do you really think you can get rid of yourself with a pencil eraser?"

"Nah," he said. His voice fell. "I just hoped my dad would notice the marks and give me some attention."

We stood there a few minutes in silence. Finally I had the courage to ask, "Did it work? I mean, did your dad notice?"

"Nope."

Maybe these are extreme examples compared to what you're experiencing in your home, but the themes are more common than you might think. What I see across the country is this: As teens seek approval and love, they'll go to extreme measures to get it from their parents—particularly their dads. If they don't get attention from their parents, they go elsewhere to get their needs met, and along the way signs will appear. Your teen may not be cutting her wrists or taking a pencil eraser to himself. Maybe it's breaking curfew, getting a tongue piercing, or wearing a skimpy dress that you disapprove of. Teens will use whatever they can to get the attention of their fathers. Sometimes teens tell me their fathers simply write off this type of behavior as "going through a rebellious stage." But I don't think defiance is the core issue with most teens I talk to. I think the issue is a cry for attention.

> **teens will** use whatever they can to get the ATTENTION of their fathers

Do you see the good news here? Hearing a cry from a teenager is an opportunity for a dad. Probably the most influential person in a teen's life, good or bad, is their father. That is why I'm writing this book! Teens want you to know: "Dad, I need you." It's so simple, but so important.

COLUMBINE IN THE NEIGHBORHOOD

In many ways my ministry right now is one of listening. But I didn't set out to make this happen. God used a horrible tragedy to bring me to this place.

April 20, 1999, was a warm spring day in Littleton, Colorado. I was a junior at Arapahoe High School, sitting in a life skills class where a guest speaker, a county sheriff, was talking to us about the dangers of drinking and driving. Our vice principal normally taught the class, but that day for some reason I could see him through the window pacing in the hallway.

It became a game to me—counting how many times the vice principal walked past the window. Five, six, seven… Boy, he must really be churning on something. Eight, nine, ten… He looked more worried than he usually did. Eleven, twelve, thirteen… I remember keeping track of his pacing with little ticks on my notebook.

Fourteen.

Fifteen.

And he stopped.

It was as if he finally found the words he was searching for. Suddenly, our vice principal burst into our classroom. I remember his statement exactly.

"There's been a shooting at Columbine High School," he said. He had tears and terror in his eyes. "They say the gunmen are coming here next."

Columbine was four miles from my high school. The kids at Columbine were all our neighbors, kids we played with on our community sports teams, kids we went to elementary school with. Our schools had a huge, good-hearted soccer rivalry. Nearly everyone in my class knew someone at Columbine.

All around me in class kids started crying. We were on the second floor, and I remember wondering how we were going to make it outside. My school immediately went into lockdown, where no one could get in or out of the building. Our principal came on the loudspeaker and gave more details. Soon we all retreated downstairs, and all the students filed into the cafeteria, where teachers were setting up a row of TV monitors. Outside, I could see a long line of parents' cars beginning to rush to our school.

I remember being able to pick out individual faces on the TV screens—faces I knew. I saw my friend Craig Nason run out of Columbine along with other frantic students, hands behind their heads so they wouldn't get mistaken for gunmen. Craig was the leader of the Columbine High School prayer group and part of a movement I helped start a year earlier called Revival Generation, a handful of students who made it their aim to begin prayer groups in every high school campus in Littleton. By then we had established thirty-five groups all across Colorado, as well as in several other states. That day I remember praying for Craig like I had never prayed before.

It's strange, the words and actions that come to you in times of crisis. As we all watched the TV screens, I remember blurting out, "We have to pray—right now!" There in the cafeteria of a public high school, in the middle of all two thousand students, a few hundred students and staff alike put their arms around each other's shoulders and formed the largest prayer circle I've ever seen within the walls of our school. Someone asked if what we were doing was legal. Someone else said, "Who cares—our friends are getting shot at."

That day was such a day of horror and confusion. Later we would learn that two teenagers, Eric Harris and Dylan Klebold, had gone on a shooting rampage inside the school. They killed twelve students and one teacher before committing suicide. Another twenty-four students and teachers were injured. Today, the Columbine massacre is considered the worst school shooting in U.S. history. For me, like so many others, that day is just one huge dark spot in my memory.

In the aftermath, so many questions were asked, including what provoked the killers and whether anything could have been done to prevent the crime. The morning after Columbine, the phone in my parents' house rang at 7 a.m. Somehow word had gotten out to the media about Revival Generation—about how a group of teenagers in the same city as the Columbine shootings had formed prayer groups. The phone rang all day long and for weeks afterward. Members of our group, including me, ended up talking to *Newsweek, Time, Oprah,* CBS, NBC, ABC, *Nightline,* a news show from Germany—all in all, forty news media appearances.

Topics of discussion ranged from social cliques in high school to feelings of helplessness, insecurity, and depression among teenagers. Anytime anyone from our group talked, we wanted people to know that whatever the reasons for this horror, there is still hope in the world—and that this hope is found in Jesus Christ.

Those were days of huge sadness for my friends and me—in spite of all the hype. Everyone sort of walked around in a fog. Yet I also believe that the Lord spoke through a bunch of committed teenagers during that time. Two friends of mine since fourth grade, brothers Steve and Jon Cohen, together with their youth pastor Andy Millar, wrote and sang a song called "Friend of Mine Columbine" at a community-wide memorial service held several days after the shootings. (Vice president Al Gore, Franklin Graham, Michael W. Smith, and Amy Grant were in attendance.)

they seemed to have unintentionally sparked a CHRISTIAN revolution

The Cohens' song talked about how guns could end dreams, but how peace and hope could be found in Jesus Christ. Jon, Steve, myself, and our friends were all used by God in great and humbling ways. Reporter Jean Torkelson from the *Denver Rocky Mountain News* said it this way: "When the two killers opened their Pandora's box of horrors, they seemed to have unintentionally sparked a Christian revolution."

God is continually teaching me the importance of availability. As His Spirit moves within my generation, it has been neat to see how He can take an insignificant guy like me and use me in significant ways. Ever since the Columbine tragedy, God has opened doors for me to speak to youth around the country an average of twice a month. Doors simply opened one by one, and I responded in faith. It's a bit crazy at times. Sometimes I'm overwhelmed. Since Columbine, I've spoken at DCLA 2000 and Creation Fest on both coasts, with the Billy Graham Association, Focus on the Family, Reach Out, First Priority, and Youth for Christ. I've been the main stage speaker at the Louisiana Baptist Youth Conference and the Wisconsin and Indiana United Methodist Youth Gatherings.

Everywhere I go, I speak with the sole purpose of helping students come to know God so that they can make Him known. Speaking at events is a God thing. It is not about me at all. I'm just a kid myself in many ways. As of the writing of this book, I'm a senior in college at Moody Bible Institute in Chicago. I'm humbled by God's calling every time I get up on stage.

I want you to know up front that this isn't a book where I aim to give any advice on parenting. Right now I'm twenty-three years old, not a parent, and I have no intentions of writing a book on a subject I haven't experienced yet. This book is about *what teens tell me.* You'll hear from real teens. Sometimes their names have been changed if the subject matter is confidential, but each of the stories I tell is true. As I speak to teens, they speak to me. And what they have to say is so important that I want you to hear it too.

From time to time in the chapters that follow, I'm also

going to weave in some thoughts from my dad, Jim Weidmann. My dad is *The Family Night Guy,* a radio show on parenting featured on about three hundred stations across the country. He also serves as executive director of Heritage Builders Ministry, a health, education, and development service for parents from Focus on the Family. He and my mom, Janet, have four kids of their own—me, my brother Jake, and my sisters, Janae and Joy. I'm the oldest. I love and respect my dad so much and I truly believe that if anyone knows something about parenting, it's him.

DaD, YOUR Teen NeeDS YOU

Think of me as a young reporter, telling you what I've seen and heard on the frontlines from the teens we both care about so deeply. In the chapters ahead, I'll tell you the good and bad of it—because I believe dads *do* want to hear what teens are saying. In fact, I believe dads must hear it, because what I'm hearing is absolutely vital to every father's success.

Dads, this is a book where you get to eavesdrop on the teen you love so much—or someone who probably thinks a lot like him or her. The bottom line from what I'm hearing is this: Dad, no matter how frustrated or limited you feel today, no one can replace you in your teen's life.

I know that meeting the needs of teens is not always easy. Often it involves *pain,* it requires *prayer,* it only comes through *patience,* and it means that dads must be *persistent.* But the rewards in family relationships and your teen's future are great. Even eternal.

If that sounds worthwhile to you, I invite you to keep reading.

THREE WORDS TO START IT ALL

"Dad, please tell me you love me."

BURIED IN THE classifieds somewhere between "Cars for Sale" and "Apartments for Rent" was a one-inch square that would shake the city of Madrid.

The ad read:

Paco, all is forgiven, please come home. I will meet you at the steps of this newspaper's office on Monday at 4 p.m. I love you, Dad.

You can guess the context of the ad by what it says—and doesn't say. It was written by a Spanish father at odds with his son. The son had rebelled and left home. The father was feeling bad and wanted his son to return, but didn't know where his son was or how to get a hold of him. So he posted this notice in the newspaper.

As the story goes, when the dad came to the newspaper steps about 4 p.m. on Monday, he was met not by his son, but by a sea of searching faces.

About two hundred young men named Paco had shown up. And every single one of them hoped it was his dad who wrote the ad and expressed his love.

IT ALL STARTS HERE

What is the absolute first thing that teens want to say to their fathers (but don't)?

It's this:

Dad, please tell me that you love me.

It sounds basic, doesn't it? Almost too simple. But it's a huge truth.

"I love you" was the first phrase I learned as a child. That's the kind of home that I grew up in. When I got up in the morning, when I went to bed, when I left for school, my parents—my dad in particular—would tell me they loved me. And I learned to say it back. As a teenager, at the end of every phone call or when leaving the house, I always told my parents that I loved them. They would reply, "We love you, too." Sometimes it felt a little weird, particularly when my friends were around, but telling my dad that I loved him was just something I did. Sometimes as I got into my later teen years, a friend would tell me I was too old to say that to my dad, but I didn't care. Dad made a habit of telling me he loved me, and I told him the same thing—it was something we were never going to change.

dad made a a habit of telling me he loved me

Here's the funny thing. The teens I talk to today seldom say to me straight up that they want their dads to tell them he loves them. They say it in sort of a reverse code. Like this:

Jenna, a fifteen-year-old I met after a talk in North Carolina, said: "My dad hasn't told me he loved me since I was a little kid. I could never come right out and say, 'Dad, I need your love.' But every once in a while I still tell him I love him, hoping he'll still say it back."

You see, in teen talk, "I love you, Dad" is more than a declaration. It's a probing question—"Do you love *me*, Dad?" And they're anxiously hoping you will say back in words and deeds, "I love you too!"

Colton, a sixteen-year-old from Illinois, told me this: "My mom tells me all the time that she loves me. My dad more shows it than says it—he and I go jogging every night after he comes home from work. Still, I wish he'd say it."

TEENS NEED TO HEAR THE WORDS

Teens tell me it's not as awkward for their moms to say "I love you." But dads are another story. Maybe we could blame it on our culture's definition of masculinity. As a boy reaches manhood, it's expected that the word *love* is something saved for mom, or perhaps a girlfriend if it's really serious. Guys certainly don't talk about *love* with other guys in the locker room, and if a guy wants to tell a buddy that he means a lot to him, he's going to be really slow to say, "I love you." Fathers are no exception.

I find that for girls this is different—they love to love. It's easier for a young woman to express her appreciation and attachment to parents, grandparents, and friends by saying "I love you."

But you know what? So many young girls tell me that their father *never* says he loves them, or that he hasn't told them he loves them since they were little. It's as if some fathers have fallen into the trap brought on by society's classification of a man when it comes to using the word *love,* even as it relates to their children. As soon as his daughter becomes a woman, or his son a man, dads don't feel comfortable saying "I love you."

The truth is, your teen is still a child inside, and he or she is facing the biggest challenges of life. They need to know *more than ever* that you love them.

DIFFICULT? MayBe
EssenTial? ABSOLUTely

Maybe you haven't told your teen you love him or her for a while. Every father has the ability to speak either a blessing or a curse into his children's lives.

My dad put it this way in one of his parenting seminars:

> As fathers we must tell our teens we love them and back it up with our actions. We dads need to know what incredible power we have in this area. Every father has the ability to speak either a blessing or a curse into his children's lives. Statistics say most male prisoners today were seldom told they were loved. To the contrary, their fathers told them they'd be a failure in life! What an example of speaking a curse.

In his seminars, Dad reminds parents that when love isn't expressed, "silence communicates confusion." When teens are left to fill in the blanks, they usually fall short on feelings of acceptance and security. That's why he and my mom aim to regularly tell my brother and sisters and I that they love us. They say it all the time, several times a day. They just weave it into the comings and goings of daily life.

If you're not much of a talker, it might feel like a big leap for you. But you can start small. Like maybe:

- Say it when you leave for work in the morning.
- Write it on a birthday card.
- Put a note on the fridge.
- Say it when you hang up the phone.
- E-mail it to your son or daughter.
- Say it when your teen leaves for a date.
- Tell your teens you love them when they go to bed at night.

Trust me, my dad is not some gushy kind of guy. He hasn't always found this easy.

"Maybe you didn't grow up with 'I love you' as part of family talk," Dad said in one of his talks. "My background is in the Air Force and in the business world. Those are two circles where men are seldom encouraged to express feelings. But now is the time to start. Dads—tell your teens you love them. Say it, say it, and say it again. Your teen may give you any number of responses when you do, but down deep it's what they absolutely need to hear."

A WOUND FOR LIFE

What happens if a father doesn't tell his teen he loves him or her? Guys and girls tell me different things here.

A daughter's need for her father's love is seen through her longing for approval. As I write this book, I have just finished traveling for seven weeks speaking at youth camps all over the United States. When I look back through my journal and recall my conversations, the number one issue I heard from teen girls was that they were struggling with eating disorders.

Statistics have shown that one in every four girls either starves herself or throws up everything she eats because she is worried about her appearance. However, in my seven weeks of travel I found that *every* girl I talked to had some sort of eating disorder, whether it was bulimia or anorexia. I couldn't believe the numbers were so high. In my conversations with these girls, I began to search for the root of their problems.

they longed
for APPROVAL
from their dads

Was there a comfort they felt from the eating disorder? A need for control? A way to get over something hurtful in their past? A lack of approval they felt from guys?

Yes to all of the above, the girls told me. But as I kept looking, at the root I found they longed for approval from their dads. Their need to control their eating was born of a lack of trust and valuation from those they love.

For years no one had shown them their true worth and accepted them. As girl after girl talked to me, once I had peeled through the layer of pain in their hearts, I would ask, "How is your relationship with your dad?" The answer always came back: minimal or nonexistent.

My aim is not to put blame on dads for the amount of eating disorders that exist in teen girls. It's a complex issue. My aim is to report back to you what I heard from the teen girls I talked to—and hurtful or missing relationships with fathers came up every single time.

A son's need for his father's love seems to be seen through his quest for acceptance and guidance.

I have a friend who has been drifting for the past four years. The ironic thing is that six years ago you would have thought this guy would shake the world. Let's call him Prodigal.

Prodigal became an Eagle Scout in high school and was headed off to a Bible college to become a pastor. Now he spends most of his time camped in an old RV in a Wal-Mart parking lot. I've asked Prodigal several times why he's chosen this path, and basically it all boils down to the relationship he has with his dad.

In Prodigal's thinking, his dad always expressed an abundance of love on his brother, but not on him. Growing up, as Prodigal got good grades, joined clubs, and kept his nose clean, his brother started smoking pot and hanging out with all the wrong friends. His brother was told he was loved; Prodigal wasn't. When Prodigal joined a band with his friends in high school, his dad told him it was a waste of time. Prodigal's dad had high hopes for him in the business world—Prodigal would succeed, end of story. But Prodigal's dreams weren't the same as his dad's.

When asked why he doesn't leave his RV, Prodigal says, "Because my dad will win." Today Prodigal is left with a pain so deep it affects the way he sees himself and the world. He fights a daily battle from a wound left by the most influential man in his life.

In his book *Wild at Heart,* John Eldridge addresses this wound that results from a father's lack of approval of who his son is…or is not. Sure, fathers have dreams for their kids. But teens tell me it's crucial that a father guides them into what *they* want to become and not what the father wants them to become. Saying "I love you," approving, and guiding go hand in hand. As Eldridge points out, this blessing on a teen's development must come from the father. When it doesn't, a teen is left to overcompensate and forever fight to get out of the shadow of the negative message engraved upon his heart.

this blessing on a teen's development MUST come from the father

Yes, a dad is faced with the tough task of showing approval, of accepting the person that his son or daughter is becoming, even if it is not who he dreamed they would be. Here's part of the way my dad is handling that with his own four kids:

"Sons need to be affirmed on who they are, given a vision on what they can become, and encouraged on how you can see them impacting the world," Dad says. "Daughters need to be affirmed on who they are, given a vision of what they can become, and told that they are attractive—so attractive that there is a prince waiting to love them into happily ever after. When I tell my two sons I love them, I also make sure they know I believe in them. With my two daughters, my love communicates my value for them."

Here's a favorite passage of mine that Heritage Builders also uses a lot. The apostle Paul commands husbands to love their wives, but he doesn't make the same command about his kids. Instead, he defines a father's love for his kids another way. In Ephesians 6:4, fathers are instructed, "Do not exasperate your children." To exasperate means to frustrate—when you frustrate your teens, you begin to push them away, and they will close off. This is the exact opposite result you desire. Dads say it's easy to become exasperated with their teens when they do things they don't want them to do. But as teens naturally try to spread their wings, I believe Scripture shows us it's best to not overparent them in an effort to show them your love.

Tim Smith, in his book *The Seven Cries of Today's Teen*, identifies five ways to exasperate a teen:

1. Judging teens by appearance or what the media tells you a teen is like
2. Sarcasm and put-downs
3. Expecting teens to act like adults because they look like adults
4. Minimizing feelings

5. Assuming that what worked when they were a child will work now

These are all negative messages that communicate "I don't love you." Your role as a father is to reverse the trends. One way to begin is by telling your teens you love them—even when it doesn't feel comfortable to do so.

THe WORDS TeeNS LONG TO HeaR

I'm blessed to say that my dad and I have a great relationship—he's on my side, not on my back. But he doesn't always agree with me. One of the areas where we butt heads most is my grades. I'll admit it, I've never been as focused as I need to be in school. I've always got too many things going on. My last year of high school I helped lead and speak at twelve student-arranged evangelistic events. I was so busy I almost didn't graduate.

Graduation for me hinged on one class—American History. I just couldn't seem to concentrate on any of the material. My dad sat me down one evening and made me sign a contract—I absolutely had to pass this class, even if it meant less time for the events. My dad and I had a long talk that night about what was important in life. We didn't agree on everything, but I remember very distinctly him telling me something again at the end of the talk. "Josh," he said, "I love you!"

Those words meant so much to me.

I studied and got a D in American History—just enough to squeak by.

And on graduation day I held my diploma high and yelled to the bleachers, "This is for you, Dad!"

tell them you LOVE them. say it, say it, and say it

Dads, you might not always agree with every direction your son or daughter takes in life, but please continue to tell them the words that bring life and healing to their souls.

Tell them you love them.

Say it, say it, and say it. Those little words change everything.

DADS IN ACTION

A CHECKLIST FOR "TELL ME THAT YOU LOVE ME"

- ☑ Remember, "Dad, I love you" also means "Dad, do you love me?"

- ☑ I don't have to be gushy! (Express love naturally.)

- ☑ Look for small, daily ways to express love.

- ☑ Three A's for Dad—whenever possible, give Approval, Affirmation, Affection.

- ☑ Cut the criticism. Stuff the sarcasm.

- ☑ "I love you!"—say it, say it, say it!

#2

A STRANGE SORT OF LOVE

"Dad, love me with actions, not just words."

LATELY, A SERIES of TV commercials has shown a strange sort of love. One opens with a group of teens hanging out in a basement getting ready to smoke pot. In the last part of the ad, a teen opens the box he hides his stash in and finds nothing but a note. It reads: "We need to talk—Mom" In another, a kid wakes up with a hangover after a night of partying. He looks in the mirror and finds "Time to talk!—Dad" scrawled across his forehead. The tagline to both commercials is:

"Parents—the anti-drug." These ads give a great picture of the second thing teens want to tell their fathers (but don't): *Dad, I need you to love me with actions, not just words.*

Setting boundaries with teens is one form of love in action. Teens tell me that even when their fathers ground them, or something gets taken away for a week or two, down deep they actually appreciate the positive attention. Isn't this how God works with us? We're told in the Bible God "disciplines those he loves, and he punishes everyone he accepts as a son" (Hebrews 12:6). God shows us His love by getting involved in our lives. Similarly, when dads give freedom and couple it with guidance, teens feel love. But too much freedom makes teens believe their dads have abandoned them. When teens feel like dads have given up on them, they give up on themselves.

give them affection in the RIGHT way

For a father to tell his teen: "I love you," then back it up with actions is one of the greatest gifts he can give. My generation is in great need of fathers who will give them affection in the right way, so they will know when the world is loving them in the wrong way. I know this is true: If teens aren't getting the love they need, they intentionally seek it anywhere they can find it.

The results are often heartbreaking.

CECILEY'S STORY

A girl named Ceciley waited to talk to me one night after I finished preaching at a youth convention. She stood with arms crossed, sort of hugging herself like she was cold or afraid. That night I had preached on the love of God, and how we can love God by giving Him our faith. I asked her if there was something she wanted to talk about.

"I can't love God," Ceciley said. She blurted it out after a pause like it had been welling up in her for some time. Over the next half hour the flood gates of her life opened. She began with her father.

"My dad's always been great," Ceciley said. "He's always told me he loves me. But, I dunno, for the past couple years I've been confused by his love."

This is what was happening: Several nights each week as Ceciley lay in bed she would hear the floor creak, and her dad would come down the hall and into her room. He would crawl into her bed and begin to slowly run his hand up her leg and touch places he shouldn't.

She began to cry as she talked.

"I thought that he loved me," Ceciley said. "But now he just uses me."

There was more.

Ceciley had met a guy her age, and they dated for about two months. She really liked him, and he seemed to like her back. He even told her he loved her and that she was special to him.

"He told me he wanted to show me his love," Ceciley said. "He said we needed to have sex and do sexual things so that we could experience that love. I didn't want to, but I didn't want to lose him either. So we did."

She was crying hard by now and gasping for air between her sentences. I was getting teary, too. I had no idea what to say to this girl. She just wanted to be loved in the right way, but was experiencing only the wrong. I asked if she had talked to her youth pastor about this. She began to cry harder.

"Yeah, I went to the church one day and met with my youth pastor," Ceciley said. "I told him about my dad and my boyfriend and what they did to me. He told me it was okay, and that God still loved me. He said he cared for me and hoped the best for my life. But then, right there in his office, my youth pastor started to kiss me. He said he loved me and ran his hands all over me. He used me! Right there in the church!"

She had anger, fear, sorrow, and hopelessness in her voice, but there was one more question she had waited to ask.

"Is God like that?" Ceciley asked bitterly. "Does God just say he loves me, then spit me out like every other man in my life?"

This poor, hurting girl. I felt so sorry for her. I didn't know if my words would mean anything, but I know God's Word is powerful. I took Ceciley to Ephesians 3:18—a passage that shows God's love is higher than the highest star, longer than the longest road, deeper then the deepest ocean, and wider than the widest sky. I told her about God's unconditional love—that He loves us no matter what. I described God's love as the deep end of a swimming pool—it's up to us to jump in and experience that love through faith.

"God's love is true love," I said. "He will never leave you, hurt you, or take advantage of you. Ever."

As Ceciley walked away that evening, I realized again that love must be backed up with actions—and the right actions— or it feels like a lie. When the actions are wrong, everyone gets hurt.

HOW DOES A DAD SHOW LOVE THROUGH ACTIONS?

Dads, as you love your teens in the right ways, you are giving them the foundation of confidence they need for life. If the need for a father's love is left unmet, it leaves a hole in a teen's heart forever. When you show your teen you love him or her, you are giving them the acceptance and security they require.

What are some practical ways a father can show love to a teen? My dad and I sat down the other day and made a list:

LOVE IS SHOWN THROUGH TIME

Teens are loved by the way you give time to them through personal involvement and conversation.

One of the most straightforward ways to give time is to be involved in school functions and youth group programs. Dads don't always have to be there, but teens say they appreciate it when their dads know what's going on. Teens also say they just enjoy hanging out when there's no agenda to discuss or appointment to be at. Your teens want to spend time with you so they can see their value in your life. They understand that if something is important to you, you will give it your time. It's vital for them to feel valued in your life and trusted with your time.

relationships with men tend to be ACTIVITY based

My dad says he's always found it easy to build relationships with his sons—he knows the way his boys are wired. Relationships with men tend to be activity based. So when my brother and I were younger, we joined the Boy Scouts with my dad. As we got older, we began to play golf and take road trips together.

But Dad says it's been harder for him with my sisters. Relationships with females tend to be conversation based. One of the things they do together now is go to coffee and simply sit and talk for hours. When they arrive home, my sisters are glowing. They feel like princesses after Dad has given them his undivided attention.

Dad purposely makes time for his children and actively seeks ways to build relationships with them. Often that means doing what they like to do, not so much what he wants to do. Sure, it was easier when we were little. Now, Dad is trying to fit into *our* schedules. Between school, work, sleep, eating, and our social lives, we don't have as much time readily available for dear old Dad. So he's found he must intentionally seek to find things we like to do with him. My fourteen-year-old sister loves to play board games, so she and my dad have about four different types of board games they play. I don't know if my dad is a big fan of games, but it provides them with an incredible opportunity to talk and laugh.

"Time is a scarce commodity," says my dad. "We only have close contact with our children for a limited period of life. Those of us with adult children know how fast time passes. Once it's gone, you can't get it back."

My encouragement to all dads is this—take the time today. When your children are grown, the bulk of daily stuff that robs you from them today probably won't matter.

THE TOUCH OF TRUE LOVE

As a son, I know one of the greatest ways my dad can tell me he loves me is through touch. Sometimes it's just a pat on the back or his hand on my shoulder, but I always know my dad loves me. Though I'm twenty-three now, my dad and I still hug each other, and often he kisses my cheek before I leave for a trip. Our masculinity isn't violated. He's my dad. I hope our hugs never change.

Touch is absolutely necessary for daughters, too. With the teens I talk to, girls say they often seek physical affection from boys when what they really want is love. But if daughters got their need for touch met from their fathers, they wouldn't seek it out from other men. Girls who are loved through touch in the right way by their dads stand stronger in the face of sexual temptation.

My dad has both sons and daughters, and he's found that expressing his love through touch to either is not without its challenges. Yet, he knows that a father's love must be expressed through the millions of small encounters that happen in everyday relationships. How love is expressed daily sets the image of God in our lives. It instills in us our ideas about manhood, about womanhood, and how we get along with other men and women.

how love is expressed daily sets the image of GOD in our lives

For his sons, my dad knows he carries the responsibility to model how God loves us, how a husband loves a wife, how a father loves his children, how a godly man lives out his life, and how godly men relate to each other and fulfill the Great Commission. Touch is a vital part of all this.

For his daughters, my dad knows he sets the image of how God loves them, how a godly husband loves his wife, and how other men should treat them. I hope my dad never stops loving his daughters the way he does now.

Author John Trent says touch is one of the critical elements in passing on a legacy of blessing, because it communicates love and personal acceptance. So, dads—please don't shy away from this responsibility of touch. Make use of every encounter to show appropriate affection.

What are some appropriate ways to show affection? Here's how it works in our home.

With my brother and me, sometimes it's…

- a "manly hug" when walking out the door.
- a hand on their shoulder or arm when dad talks with us.
- a pat on the back if we've done something well.
- a handshake when he wants to say "well done."

With my sisters, it's…

- a kiss on the cheek when they leave for school.
- a hug around the shoulder as they come off the soccer field.
- a time of holding hands as they take a walk or watch a movie together.
- just sitting on the couch with his arm around them, talking.

LOVE IS SHOWN THROUGH APPROVAL

Expressing love through approval can be tricky—what if your teen does something you don't agree with? Yet approval is the foundation of security. Approval doesn't always mean giving consent, it just means supporting someone—being on your teen's side and not on his back.

I recently talked with a girl named Shanna. When Shanna was younger, she was involved in gymnastics. Now at sixteen, she was pregnant and struggled with eating disorders, alcohol, and sex addictions. When I asked her about the relationship she had with her dad growing up, she said he was never there for her. He was always at the office.

approval doesn't always mean giving CONSENT, it just means supporting someone

"He worked hard—maybe too hard," Shanna said. "I wish he could have been around for me more. Just once I wanted him to come to a gymnastics meet and tell me I was doing all right."

"Is he involved in your life now?" I asked her.

"No," Shanna said. "I think he's too embarrassed of me."

Through the rest of our discussion, it became clear that Shanna didn't blame the life she had now on her dad, but she did talk about a void in her heart that only a father could fill.

Shanna's need, just like that of any teen, went beyond her dad's physical presence. It was a need for a positive relationship with her dad—wherever she was at in life. She needed his approval when she was younger and craved his time and now, when she is struggling, she needs his presence to help guide her. She needed him to help her see her own worth, so she didn't have to seek it elsewhere.

In my own life, I felt my dad's approval when he took interest in the things I found interesting—even when it seemed to him I came from another planet! My dad was a football player throughout high school and college. I'm sure he would've loved me to follow his steps into sports, but music became my thing.

In high school, a bunch of buddies and I started a ska-punk band called "Time for a Haircut." We'd hang out at a local teen club on weekends and dance in this style called "Skank" (basically, it's running in place while touching your toes). Concerts were always crowded with lots of pushing.

This was not my dad's thing at all! But my dad would still come to concerts with me every so often. He'd talk about music and about what was going on, trying to understand our crazy movements. I'm positive he never liked the music we played. He certainly never skanked out on the floor with us—I wouldn't have wanted him to. But he approved of me as a *person*, his son. His endorsement had a power far beyond words.

LOVE AS COMMITMENT

It's a fact: My generation is growing up in a world of broken promises. I meet a lot of kids from broken or blended families. Young people today have experienced more divorce than any generation before. One consequence is that teens are struggling with fears of being abandoned. More than ever, they want reassurance that the people they care most about will be there for them.

I address this in one of my talks called "The Promise of God's Presence." I remind teens that once we're in a relationship with Jesus Christ, He's there for us always. When I talk about this, I have everyone in the audience hold up one hand and say the following five words, matching one with each finger; "I-will-never-leave-you."

Then I asked each person to add their name. With grins on their faces, sometimes through tears, students hold their hands up and shout, *"I-WILL-NEVER-LEAVE-_____!"*

The last word is always a cacophony of noise as each student shouts his or her name: *Justin! Emily! Caitlin! Carlos! Aiden! Brandon!*

It's a beautiful thing. Students absolutely glow when they understand someone loves them and is always there for them. Dads can help teens understand this power of commitment. In a world of broken promises, teens want assurance you will not abandon them. Even if you don't live with your teen, he or she will want to know you make them a priority.

My dad has said more than once that my brothers and sisters and I are more important to him than work, hobbies, or sleep. We know he's there for us. We know his work is important, too, but we always know we come first. If he's in a meeting and we call, he's told his office assistant that she is free to interrupt. And she does. I know my dad has held up important meetings to take a phone call from me. Sometimes he even has the guys in the office say hello.

Maybe that won't fly where you work, but here are some other ways dads can show commitment:

- Remembering birthdays and Christmas with cards, gifts, phone calls, and your presence.
- Making—and keeping—promises to go on an outing your teen is looking forward to.
- Staying in the living room and watching a TV show your teen wants to watch, even when you don't.
- Meeting your teen's friends, remembering names, and asking how they are.
- Showing up on time when picking a teen up from school or practice.

YOUR LOVE EXPRESSED THROUGH GIFTS

One great way love can be expressed is through gifts. But teens tell me gifts can also backfire. I've got a friend whose dad seldom spends any time with him, but frequently slips ten dollars under his plate at breakfast. My friend has told me more than once that he'd rather have the time than the money. Gifts alone won't cut it—they have to be backed up by actions and quality time.

But gifts can make powerful statements, too. My dad is really big into giving "milestone" gifts—gifts that have a lot of meaning behind them. For each of my brothers and sisters, my dad gave us a Bible when we turned ten. When each of my sisters turned fifteen, Dad gave them a cross necklace with a diamond in it—it meant: "Welcome to womanhood." When my brother and I turned eighteen, Dad gave us gold signet rings with our initials on them. The rings symbolize a phrase Dad has instilled in us: "Walk in confidence with Christ and return with honor."

your love

can't be replaced

Gifts will not buy a teen's love. Gifts are only temporary—a teen knows that. But gifts do matter. When a dad gives a gift backed up with his love, it drives home the point that the teen is secure, wanted, and welcomed.

A STRANGE SORT OF LOVE

Dads, the second thing your teens want to say to you (but don't) is: *Dad, I need you to love me with actions, not just words.* Your love can't be replaced—it's absolutely necessary. And your actions take your love straight to your teen's heart.

Sure, actions take time, and time is precious for busy working men. But someone once said: "Never let the urgent knock out the important." You can do it. Something will always come up that seems more important than your teen. But make your personal "show-and-tell" kind of love real to your teens and you'll see important changes for the better.

DADS IN ACTION

A CHECKLIST FOR "LOVE ME WITH ACTIONS, NOT JUST WORDS."

- ☑ Realistic boundaries for your teen means love, too.

- ☑ Sexual abuse is *never* love.

- ☑ Smart dads make time, give time, show up on time.

- ☑ Appropriate touch speaks volumes.

- ☑ Keep your promises.

3

MY FATHER, MY FRIEND

"Dad, I need your friendship."

AT THIRTEEN I was convinced I was going to die.

I remember the evening well. With the bathroom door locked I stood in front of the mirror with my shirt off. It seemed lately my life had spiraled out of control. Strange tufts of hair grew over my body. My voice was creaky. Spontaneous thoughts about a warrior princess named Xena wandered through my mind.

Now to top it all off, underneath my nipples I found little hard lumps—like someone had implanted dimes in my chest. Maybe it was huge zits growing inside my upper body.

Nah—it could only be one thing—I had contracted some sort of incurable disease: tuberculosis maybe, or cancer, or leprosy. I bet it seeped into me from the floor of the boy's locker room. That place was always a haven of filth.

I ran to tell my dad.

His reply was amazingly calm in view of my crisis. "Well son," he said, "you're not dying. You're turning into a teenager."

Dad and I laugh about it now. How was I supposed to know guys sometimes get hard spots underneath their nipples? Quite a few physical changes happen to teens as they cross from childhood to adulthood, and I was the kid who worried about every one! Every day of puberty seemed like a barrage of new feelings, thoughts, and physical changes.

the relational change between you and your teen is NATURAL and necessary

With all these changes happening during the teen years, aspects of the parent-child relationship transform, too. The son you once left at home when you went to play golf with the guys from the office is now joining you as one of the men. The daughter you once took for an ice cream soda is now sitting across from you at a fancy dinner telling you about the college boy she admires. Any adjustment in life can bring fear and anxiety, but the relational change between you and your teen is natural and necessary.

Teens notice this transformation with their dads, too.

Like Danica, eighteen, from Illinois: "I ask my dad for advice a lot more than I used to," she says. "It's funny, but I find he's getting a lot wiser the older I get."

Kyle, fourteen, from California: "Sometimes my dad still treats me like a little kid. The other day we went out to Denny's, and he actually ordered for me. I just wish he would ask my opinion more."

Brianna, sixteen, from Missouri says: "The other night my dad asked me to install a computer program for him. That made me feel good. Like he really valued something I could do."

Hayden, seventeen, from Tennessee says: "My dad and I have been training for a marathon together all this year. When we're out running we have some great talks. Sometimes after a run we pray together. It's the coolest thing."

THE NEW DAD

The older my dad and I get, the more we share life on a daily basis. Sometimes it's through phone calls; sometimes it's just by hanging out together when I'm home. We talk more, and the conversation is more of a dialogue—we both ask questions of each other and share stuff. For fun, we do all the things guys do together—we go to games, play golf, and eat bratwursts, barbecued ribs, and burgers. Some people will find it a strange statement, some won't, but it's the truth—today my dad is one of my closest friends.

People define friendship a lot of different ways. Some say you should never be friends with your children—you always have to be their parent. When kids are young, I think that's true. Seldom do kids really want their parents to be buddy-buddy with them as equals. Part of a kid's security comes from the authority a parent brings. But it's also true that kids of all ages long for closeness to their parents. Teens are often as interested in what you are like, as much as you are interested in them. They want acceptance on your playing field—whatever field that is. They want to know that you think their thoughts and opinions are valid. Some call this new relational stage "companionship"; some call it "camaraderie." I describe it this way—the third thing teens want to tell their dads (but don't) is this: *Dad, I want to become your friend.*

Is friendship with your teen a hard idea to grasp? My dad describes at least four distinct parental roles that help put it in perspective:

- *Nurturer*, from birth to age 7. The primary role of a dad at this stage is taking care of his child through his provision, security, and presence.
- *Teacher*, from 8 to 15. Dads must teach kids the fundamentals of the faith, morality, and wisdom while they are growing up at home.

- *Mentor*, from 15 to 18. A primary objective at this stage is to help teens navigate culture and learn to be morally responsible adults when they leave home.
- *Friend*, from 18 to adulthood. When solid foundations are in place, kids will begin to think and function as adults and seek the advice and company of their parents.

Dad as Wally-Wally

Remember the movie *Crocodile Dundee*? There's a scene where Michael J. Dundee, the eccentric crocodile poacher from Australia, is walking through a high society party in New York. The American reporter who's brought him to the States begins to point out various people. When she comes to her psychologist, Dundee asks: "What does he do?" The reporter says: "He helps people talk through their problems."

Dundee replies, "I don't need one of them. I have Wally."

Wally was the name of a good friend back in Australia whom Dundee talked with openly—and Wally talked openly with him. Wally and Dundee shared a familiarity where they understood each other and offered perspective into each other's lives. Sometimes being a parent is like being Wally to your teen. And sometimes your teen might be Wally to you. It won't always be completely reciprocal, of course. But to move from parenting to friendship means you are companions with each other through thick and thin. A friend is someone that you can spend time with, be still with, have fun with, cry with, and enjoy life with!

Besides marriage, which I haven't experienced yet, I can't think of a better person to share friendship with than my dad. The teen-parent relationship for us was a safe and fail-safe arena in which to build a friendship. As intimacy was built and secrets were shared, neither of us was going to abandon the friendship or stop loving the other. We're family. The attachment we shared served as a safety line in case we fell. When miscommunications happened—and believe me, they did—the deep love we had in our parent-child relationship didn't let us plummet.

As your teens go through the high school years and into their college and career days, they will both make and break friendships. They will find some acquaintances that complement them as a person and others who sink them. If a strong relationship was built with a father, a teen will be able to identify the difference between a positive and negative friend. They'll also understand what it means to be a friend. Once they have joined in a friendship with another person they will better understand the ins and outs of friendship because they first shared the experience with you.

What happens when parents are anything but friends to their teens?

Last summer I talked with Kailey, a nineteen-year-old

who struggled with bulimia for most of her high school years. Every day she visited the toilet numerous times to throw up her food. She'd done it so many times she had to take medicine to calm the pain from wounds in her stomach and esophagus.

When I asked Kailey what caused her to reach the point of torturing her body, she began talking about her dad. He had always made comparisons and comments about the weight of Kailey and her sister. Even with guests in the home, he would make comments about his kids' bodies, their personality or character, or how much they ate.

her dad even made a comment about how much he DISLIKED her laugh

Kailey said one Sunday as the family sat around the dinner table with friends from church, her Dad even made a comment about how much he disliked her laugh.

"Why would he do that?" Kailey asked me through tears. "Even if something was wrong with my laugh, why'd he have to say it right then in front of everybody?"

I could still feel the pain of his comments as they sliced through the air and stabbed Kailey's heart. I couldn't believe how this man treated his daughters so ungentlemen like. The damage this father had done and was still doing was immense. Where was the support, the encouragement or rapport? He had no idea what being a friend to his teens was about.

Just as a dad's presence brings a sense of comfort to his child as a toddler, that same feeling of refuge is needed for his child as a teen. Young people today live in a world where schools, minds, hearts, and sometimes homes are battle zones. They constantly live in danger—spiritually, emotionally, and even physically. A dad's ability to get close enough to give them support and to know and encourage them to make good choices depends on his relationship with them. Through the intimacy of the relationship, dads have the ability to express and demonstrate their love and acceptance.

HOW TO MAKE FRIENDS WITH YOUR TEEN

Dads, what does it mean to make friends with your teen? Will you have to start wearing a crazy shirt or hone up on your computer game skills?

Teens say the best way to be a friend is to talk *with* them, but not *at* them or *down to* them. Worried about what to talk about? Don't! Just enter their lives and talk as stuff comes up in the natural course of life. This probably means you'll have to meet them on their playing field—and that's not always easy. If you live with a teen, you probably know firsthand how a teen can be self-centered and have ingrown eyeballs. We were all there once. But knowing that will actually help you. Because a teen is egocentric, you as a parent will probably have to be the first to bend to become a friend with your teen. This may require sacrifice on your part as a dad.

For example, I know dads who

- hate going to the mall, but go because their daughters love it.
- are not into hockey at all, but attend games and follow teams because their son loves the game.
- worry about their daughters' weight, but consistently tell them they look great, because they know this is what they really need to hear.
- give up their golf game to spend time working on their sons' cars.
- commit one night each week to spend as a "date night" with each of their children.

A huge part of being a friend to your teen is spending time where they want to spend time. Young people will typically spend their time on something that's fun and feels good to them. If spending time with their dad is something they enjoy, they'll seek it out and protect it. If it's not time they enjoy, they'll avoid it.

Even more, they'll take pleasure in the time they spend with you if they know it is something you want to do, too—*simply because you love them*. If they see that you are sacrificing something for the friendship, they'll perceive the time you spend to be of highest excellence. In the case that a sacrifice can't be made and you have to choose something over them, explain why to your teen and seek out a compromise.

Dads tell me it's also important to spend time with a teen where there is no schedule to keep and no items to discuss. There's always some sort of conversation that *needs* to happen between you and your teen, whether it is about a broken curfew, the clothes they wear, or how loud their music is. But you need times where those issues are pushed aside in order to simply build a friendship. The times that I have spent with my dad just hanging out laughing about nothing are memories I totally cherish. Teens say that in the unhurried and non-agenda times with their dads, they share some of the greatest conversations ever. Someone said once you can tell a true friend when you can sit in silence together and it's not awkward. That's built only one way—through spending time together.

When this bond is formed it cannot be broken. It will be tried and tested, but in the end it will stand firm. Years from now, this connection will be something you and your teen can fall back on.

> **you can tell** a true friend when you both can sit in SILENCE together and it's not awkward

MY FATHER, MY FRIEND

Once, when sharing this subject at a church in Wisconsin, a father came up afterwards. He had a furrowed brow and his eyes were dark, but I could tell he wanted to talk to me.

"Frankly, I'm scared to become friends with my teenage son," the father said. "If I have fun with him, he won't respect me when I lay down the rules or discipline him."

"Are you a Christian?" I asked. "Do you love God with all your heart?"

"Sure," he said, "but what does that have to do with anything?"

I pointed out several passages in the Bible, including James 2:23, that describe God's friendship with us. If God can be our friend, and we respect and want to obey Him, then certainly the same can be true in an earthy father-son relationship.

"When you're friends with your son," I said, "he'll actually obey you more, not less. You'll have trust on your side, not fear."

Teens want their fathers to be people they can laugh with about things only they would laugh about. They want a companion to share secrets and fears they would not share with anyone else. With all their new encounters in life, teens want someone that they can ask questions. Someone who won't think they're stupid for asking. This type of soul mate relationship, if built during the teen years, can produce benefits for life. If teens can open up with you while they are at home, then they'll be able to talk to you when they are at college, on their own, or when they are married.

Some of the times of friendship I remember with my dad came when I least expected it. During a simple car ride or a late night hour in the kitchen when we munched on cold pizza. These were times that never could have been scheduled or planned. In these friendship hours we'd mull over things that I was wrestling with or questioning. He would identify with me through stories and times when he had experienced the same issues and struggles. It was in the pocket of this deep relationship that I gave him a prominent platform in my life. When intimacy is shared, the power of influence is given. Now, as I'm in my last year of college, I can testify that he still has that place of power in my life. When my dad speaks into my life, what he says matters!

Dads, a deep friendship with your teens will become a strong refuge for them. They'll know it's safe to share their failures and their fears with you. When they're faced with a hard decision, they'll call on you for help. And with friendship, you can take your life-experience and the wisdom you've gained and, instead of preaching it as a parent, you get to simply share it.

Hey, that's what good friends do!

DADS IN ACTION

A CHECKLIST FOR "I NEED YOUR FRIENDSHIP."

☑ A dad gets smarter as his teen gets older!

☑ Ask your teen for advice.

☑ Becoming friends is a process (You don't have to fake it).

☑ Friendship starts with mutual respect.

☑ Talk *with*, not *at* your teen.

☑ Friends do stuff together.

☑ If you're laughing together, your friendship is probably growing.

4

NO LONGER SUPERMAN, BUT STILL a HERO

"DaD, you've always been my HeRo."

WHEN I WAS FOUR, I had a giant for a friend.

He stood twenty feet tall—I was sure of it—and he had a booming voice. Sometimes he let me try on his enormous black boots, and my feet and legs would vanish into the mass of leather. When he hugged me, my body would disappear as his massive arms engulfed me. When we walked next to each other, each of his strides matched sixteen of mine. It wouldn't take long before my little legs wore out, and the giant would place me high on his shoulders so my head was above the clouds.

"Duck," he would say, when we got to the front door of our house.

And duck I did.

As a kid it was always easy to love my dad, the giant. I never had to be taught to love him, it just happened. He was almost mythical to me—larger than life. I believed my dad could do anything. He knew everything, was all-powerful, and held my security close to his heart.

The giant was safe, too. My parents tell me sometimes I screamed at the sight of strangers, but when I was with my dad, all my fears melted. I never had to learn that my dad would protect me; I just knew it. I also understood fairly quickly that he would do anything for me; even if it meant he wouldn't give me what I wanted because he knew it would hurt me.

It seemed as if a love for my dad was planted in me from the moment I was created. Are we all this way as kids? If a love is correctly nourished, won't it naturally grow with time?

I believe it can. Here's what some teens tell me about how their love for their dads has grown:

"My dad is the coolest," says Emma, fifteen, from Oregon. "All my friends think so. He's always been a great dad, from the time I was little until now."

"Sure, I'm proud of my dad," says Rylie, sixteen, from Colorado. "He's one of the top Realtors in our city. And every Saturday when it's warm enough, we go mountain biking together. I think that means more to me than all his business stuff."

"When I was a kid, I totally thought my dad was Superman," says Austin, 18, from Nebraska. "Today, I know he's not perfect. Still, he always tries to do the right thing. If he makes a mistake, he owns up to it. I always appreciate that about him."

a hero is defined as someone who exhibits NOBLE character

"My dad's been in a wheelchair for the past two years," says Chris, fifteen, from Florida. "It's been tough on my family, but my dad has hung in there, in spite of his injury. I respect that about him."

"My dad lets me be me," says Nicki, sixteen, from Florida. "But I always know that if I step out of line, he'll talk to me about it. He never yells at me, either, like some of my friends' dads do. I like that about him."

Dad, did you know you already wear the Medal of Valor? From the get-go, God made you to be the hero in your child's life, to be the one they want to be like when they grow up.

Do you see the possibilities? I can tell you, your teens do!

A hero is defined as someone who exhibits noble character. When your son or daughter was little, you were a hero to them simply because of your presence. As kids grow older, fathers can stay heroes as they demonstrate true manhood as it relates to life, marriage, and their relationship to God. It can be done. In fact, this is the fourth thing teens want to tell their dads (but don't): *"Dad, you've always been my hero growing up. Please stay my hero now."*

HOW TO STAY A HERO

Dads I talk to say sometimes they feel pressure to be someone they're not to their teens. The dads may not be the most athletic, the greatest at their jobs, the best looking, or whatever—and they're worried they won't measure up. Dads know they're not the red-caped supermen their kids thought they were. They fear their teens' rejection as much as anything.

teens don't
expect their dads to be
TIGER WOODS

The good news is that teens don't expect their dads to be Tiger Woods or Tom Cruise. Not when they really think it through, anyway. They don't expect perfection, fame, or unusual skill; they simply want honesty, integrity, and a man of God to guide them.

How can fathers stay heroes—true heroes—in their teens' lives? My dad and I sat down and made the following list:

Love Jesus, and live like you do

Jesus Christ was the ultimate example of what it means to live in the world as a man. He did what was right, and said what He meant. Jesus was friends with rough-and-tumble fishermen. He could hold His own when debating teachers and scholars. He wasn't afraid of storms, angry mobs, or crazy people. He was tender with children, respectful of women, and took a hard-line approach to people who said they loved God but acted the opposite way.

Teens tell me the number one reason they turn away from the church is because of the hypocrisy they see within its walls. It's vital for dads to help reverse that trend by following Jesus Christ wholeheartedly. Dads can't just say they're Christians, but never act like it when they're away from church. This is what teens need to see: a man living steadily in his faith both at church and at home.

Philippians 1:27 says: "Whatever happens, conduct yourselves in a manner worthy of the gospel of Christ." When dads have Jesus Christ at the center of their lives, they can live out a genuine faith and model consistency with the Lord.

What does it mean for a dad to wholeheartedly follow Christ? Teens tell me they want to see their dads:

- Taking leadership when it comes to going to church. This isn't for just moms or kids. Dads need to be the man who gets up on Sunday morning and organizes the troops for the day.
- Reading his Bible on a consistent basis. Morning, evening, afternoon—the time isn't important, but a man needs to regularly immerse himself in the Word of God.
- Meeting on a regular basis with other godly men for encouragement, accountability, and support. Following Christ is a team effort and it takes other godly dads to walk strong.
- Living a life of integrity and honesty. Teens say that cheating on taxes or hiding a *Playboy* magazine in the bottom drawer are surefire ways to lose their respect.

By developing deep roots of faith, dads are able to be like the tree planted by water described in Psalm 1—a tree that does not wither in times of hardship, but rather produces fruit in season.

Be a Bible dad—not a TV dad

Think about the images of fathers your teens see regularly on television. Young people are infiltrated today with distorted depictions of manhood. When it comes to being a hero to your teen, you have the opportunity to set a biblical example for your children. The deadbeat dads of entertainment need to be overshadowed with the reality of fathers who live lives filled with integrity.

Biblically, the role of a man is to be a leader in the home, the pillar of faith, and the model of love for the family. Too many teens see fathers as job-obsessed maniacs, couch-loving slobs, effeminate gender-benders, or angry, aggressive competitors. What happens when men *really* live like that? Statistics point out neglected kids, frustrated wives, upset coworkers, and dangerous communities.

young people are infiltrated today with DISTORTED depictions of manhood

Your sons and daughters need you to display the true biblical essence of a man. I am still young and trying to discover all that means. But I'm grateful to have awesome examples of men in my church and with my own dad. I see dads who demonstrate integrity through their jobs. They define loyalty in how they treat their wives. Consistency is a resounding lesson I see as dads demonstrate daily care for their own body, mind, and soul.

I am learning what a man is supposed to be because I see it all around me. It's seldom found on TV. It's in the hearts and lives of dads I know who follow Christ.

Be a single standard dad

What's our character like when we're sure no one's looking? Double standards—men who say one thing then live another—are all around us. Most of us know a pastor or Christian leader who has fallen to temptation, never to get up again. Just last week I was talking with one of my best friends, Rob, who's been interning with a church youth program for over four years. Several months ago he received a shock when the youth pastor he interned under announced he was having an affair. That weekend, Rob went from intern to head honcho. He took on the responsibilities of youth pastor and picked up the shattered pieces as a hero fell and crushed the hearts of students in the youth group.

"It's hard on so many levels," Rob told me. "The bottom line is all of this mess could have been avoided."

A pastor of a college-age church I attended a few years ago went through the same experience. One Tuesday night the church packed out for the college service, same as usual, but the pastor did not arrive. Everyone just sort of milled around on the stage for about fifteen minutes before one of the church leaders arrived and informed all three thousand of us that our pastor and hero had been involved in immorality and needed to step down. What a night. Even if you're not a pastor of a large church, never question for a moment the number of people your life touches.

When a teen says, "Dad, please be my hero," he's asking you to do what you say you will, in both big and small areas of your life. The old line of: "Do as I say, not as I do," doesn't work with teens. If you're going to be a hero you must live authentically. This means holding to your word, openly admitting when you fail, but getting up and trying again and again.

Teens have an amazing ability to see through any facade. They know the difference when they are being fed a line or told the truth. Teens say they often view the church as some kind of religious country club where people come dressed to impress, say all the right things, and walk out the doors not holding to anything they just said they stood for. Ironically, young people are often more attracted to people outside the church because they view them as less hypocritical.

teens have an amazing ability to see THROUGH any facade

This grieves me! The church needs to models authenticity, just as our Savior did.

The grip of immorality and sin in families can be broken if we leave two-faced lives behind. And we must, because God is looking for men He can use, and teens are looking for heroes to model themselves after.

Aim to protect
It's almost funny to see the level of angst people go through in action movies today. Nobody lives through huge car chases,

gun battles, kidnappings, and murders and walks away the same person. After the Columbine shootings, I knew teenage friends who needed to sleep in between their parents for months because of the memories and nightmares of running for their lives. That's what truly happens when people go through a crisis. Columbine was the epitome of the dangers teens face today—physically, emotionally, and spiritually. But your teen doesn't have to experience anything like Columbine (and I pray no teen ever will again) to be in danger.

adults think

of security

DIFFERENTLY

than teens do

Car accidents, bullies, sexual assault, eating disorders—Dad has the responsibility and privilege of providing safety from all of them. A dad who protects is not only someone who provides a physical place of safety, but also a person who provides a shelter for the soul. The longing that a teen has for security ties back to a basic desire that all humans have of wanting to know that someone greater is watching out for them. This is a role tailor-made for a dad.

Adults think of security differently than teens do. Author Tim Smith explained in the *Seven Cries of Today's Teen* that, while adults find security in stock portfolios, good 401(k)s, and nice possessions, teens find security in stability, dependability, and consistency. A teen is given ultimate security when a father's actions are consistent and reliable.

What might protection look like for a teen today? Teens gave me the following definitions:

Brandi, fifteen, from Washington: "I know I can tell my dad anything, anytime, and he won't judge what I say or make me feel stupid for saying it."

Jessica, seventeen, from Georgia: "Anytime I go out with my friends my dad asks me where I'm going, who I'm going with, what time I'll be home, and if I need a ride back. I actually don't mind him asking. It sort of lets me know he's there in case I need him."

Andy, fourteen, from Montana: "I wanted to go to a dance at my school, but my dad said no. He knows I've got a couple of friends right now who only go to dances to drink."

Dads, understanding your teens' need for protection requires your involvement in their lives.

Love your teen's mom

Last summer I was a groomsman in one of my close friend's wedding. Both the bride and the groom came from broken families and they had seven parents in attendance at the wedding. This couple, Sean and Brie, have determined that they will do all that they can to ensure that they never divorce. They took all the right steps in their premarital preparation, and even now in their first year of marriage, they are setting up boundaries to give their marriage all the best odds.

Sean and Brie understand that their first commitment is to each other, and divorce is not an option in their minds. In a world where a slim minority of families are original family homes (meaning that they are not blended or broken), it's rare to find two young people like this. Because of the rising popularity of divorce over the last few decades, many teens have the distorted view that marriage is temporary. Divorce can send an unspoken message to a teen that commitment is temporary. Sometimes, they think that love can run out.

Living authentically as a biblical dad means you stick to the vows you have made to your wife. I understand that some of you may not be married to the mother of your teen, but part of being a hero to a teen means you love and respect their mother whether she's your wife or not. If you want to lose the respect of your teen really fast, start bad-mouthing their mom. Even when your teen gets angry with her, or voices bad feelings towards her, you need to be the bigger man and support her. If you treat your wife (or their mom) with respect, they will follow your lead, and their regard for you will grow.

My dad will often say that the way a dad can show love to a teen is by loving their mother. The Bible commands dads to love their wives as Christ loved the church. How is your wife's countenance—does she feel cherished, important, and valued by you?

ALONE IN THE CARD SECTION

Every Father's Day I give my dad a card that says something like: "Dad, even though I've grown up, I still look up to you." I want my dad to know he's not just my father or friend, he's my hero.

He was my hero when I was young. Dad was the giant who lifted me on his shoulders. And Dad stayed my hero when I got older. When a clerk gave my dad a few cents too much in change, dad returned to the store to correct it. More than once, he stopped by the side of the road to help people change tires or give a jump start. During winters he shoveled snow off elderly neighbors' driveways. By observing his little decisions, I knew he lived wisely in the big decisions. The way he conducted his life brought security to mine.

What's interesting to me today is how I'm often alone in the card aisle before Father's Day. Maybe because the card selection is always half what it is for Mother's Day? Or maybe it's because some people are trying to forget this holiday. The truth is, the world is full of fallen heroes. Many are fathers who have lost the respect of their children.

But great fathers still exist. There are still men that have sons that look up to them and strive to be like them. There are dads whose daughters watch them to see what a real man is like so they know what to look for in a husband.

As a father, you have a unique opportunity to be the hero

to your teen. Your position of influence in their life allows you to model authenticity and a right relationship with God so that they have an example to mimic. Please, for the sake of my generation, strive to live authentically every day. Love them unconditionally, respect their mother, and follow the Lord wholeheartedly. Give your teen and other young people someone they can still look up to.

That's what everyday heroes do.

DADS IN ACTION

A CHECKLIST FOR "DAD, YOU'VE ALWAYS BEEN MY HERO."

- ☑ Every dad starts out as a giant to his kid.

- ☑ Heroes lead the charge toward what really matters in life.

- ☑ You can't be a hero without integrity.

- ☑ Heroes use their strength and influence to protect, not exploit.

- ☑ Love your teen's mom.

5

AnYWHERE a GREEN CHAIR

"DaD, I neeD you To LISTEN"

IN THE BASEMENT of our house sits The Cave.

And in the cave sits The Chair.

The Cave is actually my dad's office. It'll never win any interior design awards. The walls are just two-by-fours. Dad scrounged an old metal desk from a dumpster years ago and it's stayed ever since.

The Chair is the only relic left over from Dad's bachelor days—Mom made him throw away all the rest. It's sort of a seasick green color with a flowered ivory weave. It's high-backed and itchy; definitely a chair you'd curl up in. Dad screwed a board on the bottom so we wouldn't fall through when we sat down.

I get dibs on it some day. I love that old hunk of fabric and steel.

The Chair was always open. Any time any of us kids wanted, we could descend to the basement, plunk ourselves in the green chair, and unleash the concerns of our soul to Dad. It became an unwritten rule in our family that anytime one of us would sit in The Chair, Dad would stop what he was doing and converse with us about the subject of our choice.

I remember one day during my sophomore year of high school when the hours couldn't go fast enough. I couldn't wait until Dad retreated into his office that night so I could go to The Chair. That morning in biology class we had studied human reproductive systems, specifically the female anatomy. My mind overflowed with questions. I knew I couldn't ask my buddies at school—they were just as confused as me. There was no way I was going to talk to my mom—she was a girl. My queries simply had to be unraveled in The Chair. After dinner that night, Dad went to the basement, and I followed on his heels.

"Dad," I began. "This morning the teacher put this chart up on the wall...."

The talk that night was not the only one of its kind. Many of my visits to the green chair involved questions about girls. Other times I wondered about God, or simply about growing up. The green chair was more than just a wrestling mat for my problems; it became my sanctuary, a podium to rest my heart on, a safe garden of growth for me mentally, spiritually, and emotionally. More than anything, the times in the green chair deepened the roots of my relationship with my dad, preparing me for a lifelong openness with him.

DAD, LEND ME YOUR EAR

Teen years are all about brand-new experiences. Questions pop up all over. Plus, your sons and daughters live in a world of overload. That means they're desperate to be heard. Having a safe place to talk—some sort of green chair—is so important for a teen. I never expected that my dad would be able to answer all my questions when I went to sit on The Chair; I just needed someone who would faithfully listen.

my dad showed me the difference between LISTENING and hearing

And he did.

A recent survey asked teens, "If you don't talk to your parents, why?" The highest response was, "Because my parents don't listen to me." Ouch!

In The Chair, my dad showed me the difference between listening and hearing. Listening involves paying attention and processing what is said to encourage, guide, or challenge my thinking. Hearing is just the process of letting me talk while his mind was elsewhere—that seldom happened. My dad always strived to really listen to me. After I spoke for a while, he could summarize what I'd just said. He became a "student" of me, often studying me with great intensity. He'd listen to my hurts, frustrations, hopes, and dreams. Listening was another way he showed his love.

Teens need to be listened to—it's absolutely essential—but many teens don't have this resource in a parent. I believe the fifth thing teens want to say to their dads (but don't) is this: *Dad, please listen to me.*

Here's what some other teens are saying about this need:

listening was
another way he
SHOWED his love

"It took awhile for my dad to get it that he didn't have to solve all my problems," said Meghann, fifteen, of North Carolina. "But now he's really good at just listening without trying to offer advice all the time. We go out to Dairy Queen almost every week. I get an Oreo Blizzard and he always orders a marshmallow sundae. Then we talk."

"My dad just yells," said Jamie, sixteen, of Minnesota. "The other day he said I couldn't go out four-wheeling because I wasn't done with my homework. I didn't have that much and I could have done it later, but he wouldn't listen. That made me mad."

"There's no way I'd tell my dad about the crush I have on

Seth," said Julia, fourteen, of Georgia. "All he ever says to me is, 'Talk to your mom.' But I don't want to talk to her. She's not my real mom, anyway."

"My dad and I play floor hockey with roller blades over at our church," said Doug, fifteen, of Ontario. "We have a key so we can go really late when there's no one around. Sometimes when we're done playing we talk about stuff as we skate around the gym."

"My dad's always been able to talk to my sister, but not to me," said Brad, seventeen, of Florida. "He played basketball in high school, so does she—I guess they have that in common. I wish I could talk to him more, particularly now that my girlfriend's pregnant. But he says even less now. Good thing I just got a job at the door factory. Now I'll be able to make some money."

But maybe listening feels impossible or like a waste of time with your teen. Maybe you've placed several "green chairs" in your son or daughter's life and you're still waiting for them to sit down.

What are some of the keys to knowing how to listen to your teen? My dad and I came up with some suggestions that have worked for a lot of other dads and teens:

Listen for the heart, not just the words

When teens ask you to listen, what they really want is for you to get involved in their lives. Listening may begin as shooting the breeze, but chances are, it'll go deeper soon. For teens to ask you to listen to them is really a plea for heart-interaction. The teen is pleading with you, "Dad, please get involved in who I am." They want your participation on an emotional level as they experience life for the first time.

Think about all that teens go through between ages thirteen and nineteen. They may experience bewilderment due to hormonal fluctuations, fear over the future, anxiety from a new job, stress from any of the many pressures at school, or more. All these new experiences can overflow young minds and hearts—and anything new will produce some sort of emotion. Here's where it can become tricky because the emotion you see won't always match what a teen is saying—at least in your mind, anyway.

the emotion you see won't always MATCH what a teen is saying

In a teenage mind, feelings can often outpace the facts they represent. For my dad, this demanded a lot of patience and added sensitivity when he listened to me. More than once I came to my father in some sort of blurry state of emotional upheaval. I had to share what was on my heart, as well as what was on my mind. And whatever was on my heart at that time was bound to be huge! For my dad, it was often easy to see through my feelings, and the solution appeared as plain as a sunny day. Still, it was important that he didn't downplay my feelings—however bizarre they may have sounded. I wanted him to listen to my heart, not just my words.

Understand what's real in a teen's world

I've met Josh McDowell at several speaking engagements, and we've struck up a friendship. Once I was driving with him to his Colorado cabin. On the way up the windy roads we talked about the confusing emotions young people often experience, sometimes even over small things. He said it best: "We need to realize that puppy love is real to the puppy." He was right! From romance to fear, if we can grasp how real feelings are to a teen, we'll be better equipped to help them work through any issues they face.

Dads, there is really nothing you can do to change a teen's emotions. Sometimes teens come to you with problems they believe are huge. Insurmountable even. To an adult mind, the problems may be nothing. That's not uncommon at all. Teens can take what looks like a flea-sized problem and make it bigger than a dinosaur in their minds. Their emotions then follow suit, which in turn can play out in their actions. And actions can be all over the place.

Have you ever listened to your teen giving what seemed like an overblown account or proposing an illogical decision, only to echo back a message of disbelief and judgment?

- "Your youth pastor hates you? Are you sure? Just last week you said he was the coolest guy ever."

- "What do you mean you're never going to talk to Melissa again? All she told you was that she likes the same boy you do."
- "You want to drop out of high school because no one asked you to the dance?"

Actually, the parent's reactions in all these statements make a lot of sense. But they miss the point—all emotions are valid for whoever is feeling the emotion! And if these kinds of reactions set the tone for what the parent says next, they'll probably do more harm than good. Bottom line: Let your teen talk without immediately lowering the boom. The environment of listening and receptivity you establish will go a long way toward helping the teen figure out his or her own solutions.

let your teen talk without immediately lowering the BOOM

Of course, the time for clear-headed—maybe even startling—feedback needs to come sooner or later. During his teen years, my brother Jake had an emotional tie to everything that tended to dictate his mood and actions. If he had his heart set on something, he would talk about it, daydream about it, and even plan life around it.

Once, when Jake was about thirteen, he got really big into yo-yo tricks. He became pretty good and would hold yo-yo shows for family and friends. In a catalog he saw something he thought he absolutely couldn't live without—a yo-yo hol-ster—something to keep your yo-yo strapped to your belt in when not in use. Jake became obsessed. He absolutely had to have the holster.

My dad thought the holster could wait. He informed Jake it was nothing he needed to continue pursuing the craft of fine yo-yoing. But Jake wouldn't quit. He begged. He whined. He sweet-talked and cajoled. It went on for hours. Finally, my dad had had enough. He uttered the phrase that became a family classic for years to come:

"Jake, the horse is dead. Dismount!"

For any teen such as Jake, strong emotions can become the magnifying glass through which he or she sees life. For my dad, even though he put the brakes on Jake that time, he knew that strong emotions—even for something as simple as a yo-yo holster—are real and justifiable for the teen. Patiently, he listened. And listened. But Jake would have held on for-ever.

At times like that, ask God to give you your own family classic!

Patience Comes Before Solutions

In our family it didn't take long for my dad to learn that you can't race to the solution. It's best to help kids to find it on their own—usually slowly—by listening. This is especially true with my sisters. When they share their hearts, the thing that causes them to continue to share is the attentiveness of my dad. I've seen him talk to them. Sometimes that's all he does is ask questions.

But other times, after my sisters finish sharing, they'll ask my dad: "So what do you think?" This is his cue. The question flings open the door to my dad's wisdom. He doesn't have to force advice upon them because they've asked him for it!

Dads I respect say that if they are patient and truly listen, their son or daughter will continue to open up and be vulnerable with them. If the dads don't listen and are quick to speak, they muffle their teen's emotions, and the teens will quickly put walls around their hearts and not allow the dads in.

Dads that I respect say there are great benefits to simply listening or asking questions before speaking. Listening allows you to get on their level and help you understand where they are and what is going on in their minds. It better prepares you when they do ask for your advice. You'll know better how to meet their need and identify with them because you have first heard their heart. You'll discover as a parent what guides your teen's thoughts. You will be able to hear the words behind the words and uncover what influences their mind and who is influencing their hearts. By listening to them, they will then be ready and more willing to listen to you. They will receive your words, and even ask for them, because you took the time to listen to them. Your teen wants to know what you think *after* they share with you what they think.

My dad often says in his seminars how valuable it is to be able to influence teens in their decisions. Teens are faced with new experiences and opportunities (good and bad) that challenge their emotions, reasoning, dreams, and decisions. The problem is that they often have limited understanding and applied knowledge with which to make the best choices on their own. Teens will often try to develop their identity and what they stand for by "testing" their ideas and opinions. The chance to express themselves gives them value because they feel that what they have to say matters. This is one of the greatest times for a parent to mentor their young adult, says my dad, through listening and guiding their decision process as they face these new daily "trials and breaks" in life.

the chance to express themselves gives them VALUE

LISTEN WITH PRESENCE, NOT JUST EARS

My high school friend Craig told me that after the shootings at Columbine he didn't remember any of the comforting words his parents said to him—not a one—*but he remembers that they were there.*

Presence is one of the most powerful ways dads can listen to teens. Some dads aim for quality time with their teens. They think that if an event is right, a memorable moment will also happen. This is sometimes true, but I think the best quality times come from large quantities of time. When you're around your teen a lot—not just in planned experiences, but through all evenings and weekends when just regular stuff happens—that is when teens will often speak the most important things.

A dad is a God-given partner to walk alongside a teen through his or her life. A teen simply longs for you to be there, but not to be preached at, for they have enough to try and grasp already. They want someone that they can vent with about what they are experiencing.

LOOK FOR SURPRISING OPPORTUNITIES

Have you ever noticed that opportunities for listening come along at the times you least expect? Here's what some of the teens have told me:

"My dad's a leader in my youth group," said Gary, fourteen, from South Carolina. "One night after a concert I got sort of choked up outside near the vans. My dad pulled me aside and asked me what was up. I told him I missed my friend, Tyler, from fourth grade. We haven't lived near Tyler since we moved five years ago. My dad just listened. Really, I think I miss Tyler because I haven't been able to make many friends since I switched schools this year."

"It sounds sort of silly," said Carly, thirteen, from Iowa, "but my dad still reads to me at night before I go to sleep. We've been reading all the Narnia books again—he read them once to me when I was little, too. It seems like there's a lot more in them about God this time."

"The other day my dad and me stopped at the grocery store," said Nicky, fifteen, from California. "He said we were in a hurry and to stay in the car. But I really wanted to come inside. He said no and got sort of angry. So I stayed. Later, when he came out, he apologized for yelling. On the ride home we started talking about when he was young and his dad used to get mad at him. Now I know why he acts the way he does sometimes."

opportunities for listening come along at the times you LEAST expect

"I've been helping my dad build our new house," said Ryan, sixteen, of Washington. "We spent all last week on the roof. While we're hammering away, he always asks me questions about God, about what I'm reading in the Bible and stuff. He makes me think a lot."

The more you spend time with your teens, the more

you'll find opportunities to talk. Sometimes a question or two needs to be asked, sometimes not. And if your teen doesn't talk, that may be just fine, too. He knows you're there, and when he wants to talk, chances are good he will.

ANYWHERE A GREEN CHAIR

I'm not at my parents' house as much as I was when I was a teenager, but whenever I'm home, I still make use of The Chair.

The other day I was wrestling with a business decision—I had thought about opening a coffee business, but I'm still in school, and my studies and speaking engagements take a lot of time. After dinner, Dad went downstairs, and I followed on his heels.

The chair is as scratchy as it ever was. It's still lumpy in the cushion. The high back sort of pushes your head forward when you lean against it.

But I talked.

And Dad listened.

I still haven't reached a conclusion about the coffee business, but my thoughts are a lot clearer since I talked with my dad. No matter how the business turns out, I know he supports me. Years of talks in The Chair have done their work.

DADS IN ACTION

A CHECKLIST FOR "I NEED YOU TO LISTEN."

- ☑ Why not make a family memory of listening *well*?

- ☑ Patient listening comes before solutions.

- ☑ Listen to the heart, not just the words.

- ☑ Look your kid in the eye.

- ☑ Give your *full* attention (your teen is worth it).

6

THE POWER OF YOUR OWN STORY

"DAD, JUST BE REAL WITH ME."

He was tall and a bit stooped. Over his left eye ran a jagged scar.

"My name's Tom," he said. His voice was shaky, like he had a lot on his mind.

Tom was one of the dads at a men's prayer luncheon. I had just finished talking to the fathers about what teens wish they could say to their own dads.

"It was that point you made about being real with your teen," Tom said. "That was tough for me to hear. I just don't know if I can do that with my daughter. I don't want to completely lose her…."

Tom began to tear up at this point. He explained that he had just spent a year in jail. His past was checkered by drug use, immorality, and drunkenness. But in jail he had found a relationship with Christ and was now living a transformed life.

"What I'm afraid of is this," Tom said. "My daughter doesn't know where I've been this past year. I think her mom told her I was traveling. I'm scared that when my daughter finds out the truth she won't respect me anymore. I just don't know if I could handle that."

THE TRUTH OF YOUR LIFE

Tom raised a great question: how much of your previous experiences and day-to-day struggles do you share with your teen? How would a teen answer Tom's question? I believe the sixth thing teens want to tell their dads (but don't) is this: *Dad, please be real with me.*

Teens tell me they want to know the truth. They want to see and know an authentic father. It's also true that they may not need or even want to know every detail of where you've been and are. I encouraged Tom to go and share with his daughter about where he had fallen in the past and to tell her the truth about his time in jail. I warned him not to share it all at once, but in time to allow his daughter to know her dad better and learn from his mistakes. Authenticity demands vulnerability. Raising a teen means you must begin to open the vault of secrets in your own life, not just to air the laundry, but also to guide them and help them to avoid the mistakes you made.

When I speak to teens about what it means to be real, I share three vital areas of honesty that help expose the truth about who they are. I tell them we must first be honest to God, about who He is and who we are in Him. Second, I share that we must be honest to ourselves about who we are and not just who people tell us we are. Lastly, I talk about the way we need to be honest to the world, living life boldly and our faith shamelessly. In the end, it simply comes down to living honestly. Just as your teen has asked that you be genuine with them, your example and insights into their life will help them understand that authentic living gives way to a true identity.

teens are quick to notice a FACADE

Teens are quick to notice a facade. If you hide from them, they will hide from you. Teens want you to share not just good points or wise sayings, but real stories…about you. They want to know that you have faced what they face. When you tell your teen real life stories, you'll be able to connect with them in a much better way than any three-point sermon.

My dad tells his parenting seminars that one lesson he and my mom have learned from their children is that vulnerability is a key to intimacy. If parents are vulnerable with their kids, they will be vulnerable with you. My mom and dad have tried to share their pasts—both good and bad experiences—in an effort to guide us kids so we make similar good choices, and don't make the same mistakes. Their discussions with us center on the decisions they made, why they made them, and also on consequences that still impact them today. Teens need to understand that some of the choices they make today can have lifelong emotional and physical repercussions. By helping teens focus on consequences, a dad's desire is to equip his teen with the foreknowledge that will keep the teen from falling.

but how do you know what to share and what NOT to share

But how do you know what to share and what not to share?

My dad says his bottom-line criteria involved knowing where his kids were. By knowing our spiritual, emotional, and social maturity levels, he only shared what he believed we were ready for. He never told us stories to glorify his past—particularly when at times his past didn't glorify Christ. His aim with any story was that we'd learn from it. He'd also qualify stories by repeatedly telling us that choices have consequences, and that God's plan for our lives involved us following Him wholeheartedly.

PASSAGE TO ADULTHOOD

What is one key to knowing where your teen is really at in their progression to adulthood? It can be tougher today because, unlike many other cultures, our western society has few ceremonies to mark stages of maturity and development. In some African tribal groups, every teenage male will have to kill a lion before being accepted as an adult. Other cultures treat the onset of menstruation in young women with great respect and celebration. One huge benefit of the ceremonies is that they are clear and unambiguous—and the message is public. Before the ceremony happens, you're a kid. After it happens, you're an adult.

A rite of passage is one way you as a parent—and the culture your family stands for—can pass on your story to the next generation. The ceremonies and celebrations formally recognize, accept, and welcome the young person into adulthood. But they also serve as a record of identity—"this is who I am"—and can help to make your teen's heritage real and powerful to him or her in the years ahead.

The closest things we have in North America to right-of-passage ceremonies are getting a driver's license and graduation. In the south they have debutant balls. That's about it. Even then, teenagers with driver's licenses are hardly thought of as grown up. It seems we have a lengthy slide into adulthood in this society.

I think there's a lot to be said for churches and families creating right-of-passage ceremonies for their teens.

In my family we've created a ceremony like this. We don't have a formal name for it, but it's sort of like a Christian bar mitzvah. It occurs in two stages. The first is a weekend away with mom or dad when we turn twelve. My sisters would each go away with my mom, and my brother and I went away with my dad. It was a good time. We'd go somewhere that meant something to us, a nice hotel or out camping. We ate good food and did something fun together. We'd also have a lot of time to hang out and talk.

one of the greatest deceptions of the culture is the MEANING of sex

For that weekend, my parents would create the right context, now that we had reached the right maturity, to share with us in the right way about sex and the need for abstinence. These were weekends of information, warning, encouragement, and preparation, but most of all authenticity. My parents' vulnerability was the power that equipped us as children to face the choices that they once faced themselves.

Part two happened when each of us kids turned fifteen. We called this our "Rite of Passage" time. For six weeks each of us kids did a Bible study every night with either our mom or dad. We'd talk over role models, choices, and what it means to be a godly grown-up. Each week we also had to identify six adults we knew whom we considered role models. Each adult needed to exhibit a different characteristic. Like one had to be a good leader, another had to be a good listener, etc. Then we would call each of our role models at the end of each week to ask questions and ask them to pray for us. Again, my parents' vulnerability during these times was so important. Sometimes, the Bible studies would just turn into talks where my dad shared stories of his life.

ReclaImIng The GIFT—anD ResponSIBIlITIes—oF sex

I often speak to teens about sexual temptation and how open-sexuality is the cancer in the souls of many people. My primary passion in life is to go share the gospel of Jesus Christ with young people, but there is such an epidemic of sexual obsession among teens that I feel I continually need to address this area of their lives.

One of the greatest deceptions of the culture is the meaning of sex. What our society promotes and has legalized is not always moral. But God created sex and blessed it in the union of two people committed to each other—legally and lifelong. My dad always stresses in his seminars that teens need to know why God created sex only for marriage. The purpose of abstinence programs is not just to prevent teenage sex, but also to guide young people to a greater intimacy once they marry.

Unfortunately, immoral sex is the god of this generation;

it is the drug that more and more teens are experiencing at younger and younger ages. Teens tell me that sex has truly lost the characteristic of intimacy and is now considered merely a social encounter between two people. We could blame it on Hollywood, commercials, magazine ads, or politicians, but it doesn't really matter what spreads it, what matters is who is countering it.

What have I heard in this arena? You wouldn't believe it.

- I had a thirteen-year-old boy tell me that every day after school he goes to a friend's house with a group of guys. They gather around the TV and watch a porn video while they all masturbate together.
- A fifteen-year-old told me all the kids in his grade simply refer to sex as *hooking up*. "Sex is about as casual as dating," he told me. "It's sort of expected that you *hook up* with a person if you've gone out with them once or twice."
- Last winter I spoke at a camp in Wisconsin where two sixteen-year-old girls told me they decided before coming to camp they were going to lose their virginity that weekend. When asked why, they said because they had no reason not to. I asked them if they were scared of getting a disease, or pregnant, or caught by their parents. They said there was no consequence that scared them enough to keep them from doing what they planned.

- A seventeen-year-old told me all her friends were very interested in lesbianism. "It's sort of the new cool thing to do," she told me. "I kissed a girlfriend at a party last week. I didn't like it, but I'm glad I tried it."
- Two middle-schoolers told me a group of their friends had been gathering behind their school for several weeks to experiment with oral sex. Everyone at school knew about it, but nobody seemed to think it was that big of a deal.

Surely one of the critical issues to address with teens is the consequence of their sexual choices. Teens tend to have a sense of invincibility—they believe nothing can happen to them—ever. It is because of this that they need your vulnerability. A teen might not listen to statistics of what could happen if he or she makes the wrong choice, but teens will remember stories you tell them of your past when you were faced with a similar decision.

Whether you chose the right way or fell into the temptation, either way your story will inspire them to run, or give them a warning if they're about to fall.

Still, the most important help against temptation is not consequences, but fear of the Lord. When Potiphar's wife tempted Joseph to come to bed with her, he told her: "How then could I do such a wicked thing and sin against God?" (Genesis 39:9). Fear of the Lord means a teen learns to respect the righteousness of God. Your personal story alongside the commands in Scripture will set them up for the best success when standing face-to-face with sin. When teens want to understand how far is too far physically, you can lead them to Scriptures like Ephesians 5:3. Here God's Word is clear that His boundary for sexual immorality is "not even a hint." To show this Scripture to them, not in a sermon, but in a story from your life, will strongly prepare them to set high standards with a boyfriend or girlfriend.

What are some examples of success that I've seen in this arena? Listen to some of the teens I've talked to:

"My dad dated a lot of people before he met my mom," said Andrew, fifteen, of Oklahoma. "But he decided he wouldn't kiss my mom until he proposed to her. On the night he proposed he told her he loved her for the first time, and then they kissed. They were married six weeks later. I think that's so cool."

"When my dad was in college he got engaged twice," said Curtis, eighteen, from California. "But I know he never had sex with either girl because he told me."

"My mom doesn't give me very many details about the guys she dated before she met my dad," said Hannah, fourteen, of Texas. "But she always tells me never to date someone just because I want a boyfriend. She did that a couple of times and it never turned out good."

"I know my parents 'did it' before they were married because their anniversary date is only five months away from my birthday," said Mick, seventeen, of Pennsylvania. "They say they were happy to have me, but it sure was tough to be so young and have a kid. I guess that's always made an impression on me to wait."

Real You, Real Redemption

Dads, your teens want you to be real with them, but with knowledge comes responsibility, and you must make sure that they are ready to handle it. Sharing from your past must come in the right way, in the right context, and with the right maturity in the child. Giving your child responsibility through knowledge, as they are ready for it, will better equip them for the road of life on their own.

For my dad, I know one of the reasons he was scared to share his past with us was that he feared we would use it against him. He didn't ever want us to go and experience something he had told us about and then say: "Well, Dad, you did it when you were my age." My dad will tell us stories about his past and always qualify then with the statement: "That was B. C." (Meaning *Before Christ*). He always wanted to make clear that his mistakes were before he had a relationship with Christ and his life had been changed. And we kids respect this. There's sort of an unspoken pledge to not use anything Dad did "B. C." against him.

Dads, as you open your heart on the issues of your life, your teens will open their minds and be able to make wise decisions because they were prepared with your wisdom. Being real is the most effective way to shepherd a teen's heart. And it opens the door for God to share the redemption that's happened—and still happening—in your life with your child. Of course, vulnerability on any level is hard, but I encourage you to ask God to show you how to use the truths of your life to prepare your kids in important ways for the road ahead.

DADS IN ACTION

A CHECKLIST FOR "JUST BE REAL."

☑ Your life story (even the bad parts) has great power for your teen.

☑ Live and speak honestly—teens can spot a fake.

☑ Be sensitive about what your teen is ready to hear.

☑ You have to bring up the subject of sex and teach what matters, otherwise all the other (probably destructive) influences will prevail.

☑ Redemption changes people. (Spread the news!)

7

GETTING READY FOR THE GAME

"DAD, PLEASE BE MY COACH."

In my teen years, I caught myself sounding a lot like I did when I was five.

I'd still look in the mirror and say *ragafrazzalmazzledazzal.*

I'd still eat cereal in the morning and say *uhummmm.*

I'd still sit behind the wheel of a car and say *rummmmm-rummmm-rummmmmmm.*

And one of the word-for-word phrases I said in both seasons was this: *I can do it myself.* It was an announcement of independence—I was old enough to figure stuff out on my own. Sound familiar?

But here's the funny part about that phrase: As much as I cried freedom, I still wanted my dad in my life. I wanted to fly, but I also desperately craved his safety net in case I crashed.

Recently in the mall near my college, I saw a little kid walking along a low curb with his dad. As the child balanced, his dad held his hand. The child said: "Daddy, I can do it myself." And the dad let go. Yet as the child continued to walk, the child kept his hand lifted over his head as if still holding his father's hand.

during the influence stage, your teen is looking for a whole DIFFERENT fathering approach

That was it! What a great picture of me in my teenage years. I wanted self-determination, but I wanted my dad's presence, too. For years I have heard my dad talk on the bell curve of relationships in a child's life. It helps me understand the "I can do it"/"I need your help" paradox. Here is how it works:

The left side of the curve (the rising side) is called the "imprint stage" of a child's life. Here, kids believe what you believe or because you tell them to believe. The time period is usually from birth to age seven, until they hit the age of reason.

From ages seven to fifteen (the "bell" of the curve) is

called the "impression stage." During this time, kids seem to be most receptive to your values and beliefs as they begin to think things out for themselves.

In latter teen years, about ages fifteen to eighteen, (the downward sloping of the curve) kids move into the "influence stage." Here kids tend to seek independence and become less receptive to parental values and beliefs as they begin to test and determine their own. The teens in this stage still want you around, they just want to figure stuff out on their own.

During the influence stage, your teen is looking for a whole different fathering approach. And it is described in what I believe is a seventh thing teens want to tell their dads (but don't): *Dad, please coach me.*

DaD, THE FamILY COaCH

What is a coach, and why should you be one to your teenager?

A coach is someone who guides and directs by walking alongside—not by carrying the other person. You can teach your children about life, but the real learning comes when they have to apply what you have taught.

That is what teens are seeking—the opportunity to experience life as you have prepared them for it. They want the security of knowing you are there—not micromanaging their every step, but standing close ready to catch them if they fall.

Here's how some teens have explained this need to me:

"My dad absolutely freaked out when I was driving the other day," said Brandon, 16, of Wisconsin. "He was sure I didn't have the car in gear, but it was totally in gear. I knew it and told him so. I just wish he'd relax more and know that I can do this."

"I wrote my cousin a letter because my aunt and uncle are going through a divorce right now," said Marianne, seventeen, of Pennsylvania. "My mom said I shouldn't—that I should just stay out of things. But my dad said he knew I could handle it. I wanted to tell my cousin everything was going to be okay."

"Everyone in my youth group is going to Mexico this summer on a missions trip," said Johanna, fifteen, of British Columbia. "But I can't go because my dad says it's too dangerous. I don't think it is—my youth pastor takes kids there every year."

"I took AP English this semester even though I wasn't sure I could handle all the reading," said Mark, sixteen, of Illinois. "My dad said he'd be there to help me if I needed it. The class was tough, but I did okay."

Dads, you might have a hard time thinking of yourself as a coach. But your teenagers are used to relating to coaches, mentors, and tutors—people that help them when they need it. Your teens count on this for success.

After my dad graduated from the Academy, he stayed on as football coach before heading off to flight school. He said one of the most interesting things about coaching was that you spend about ten hours on the practice field each week for each four-hour game. Most of practice time is spent running plays against an opponent's different formations. When game time came, players had already experienced an opponent's moves.

Dad says parenting is like this, too. When a child becomes a teen, dads move into a coaching role. During practice (when a teen is still under your roof) a coach will be on the field with the players, giving them individual attention and guidance. The home is the practice field. Dad, the coach, is there watching, listening, directing, encouraging, and correcting.

when a child becomes a teen, dads move into a COACHING role

During game time, coaches stand on the sidelines providing input only when players come off the field. My dad says "the game" is when teens leave and go to college, get a job, get married, or move away. Then, young adults will be forced to apply what parents have taught. They may also discover what wasn't taught. Dads need to spend their "practice" time developing and expanding a teen's responsibility levels so they can succeed as spiritually, emotionally, and socially independent adults in the game of life.

I recently heard our pastor say that God's Word *teaches* us God's will, but we truly *learn* it when we have to apply it. This is what I have come to understand as the difference between being a teacher and a coach. A teacher presents the principles that guide our life; a coach helps us to apply them in the everydayness of life. This becomes so important during teen years when young people seek their own identities and values. When teens are in the heat of combat and competition, they need more than a head full of knowledge. They need trained reflexes and trusted experience. Good coaching delivers exactly that.

PUNTS, PLAYS, AND PASSING FORMATIONS

Teens tell me there are two main areas they look to their dads for coaching help in—relationships and life skills.

So much of life revolves around relationships—it's how we relate to people and they to us. Relationships involve

- how we treat the grocery clerk when we have to stand in line.
- how we talk to our boss if we don't agree.
- how we get along with our roommates at college.

- how we follow our pastor's leadership.
- what we look for in a best friend.
- who we marry until death do us part.

And so much more.

My seventeen-year-old sister's best friend right now is a guy. It's interesting to listen to my dad talk to her about their friendship. He encourages it, yet guides her in what to watch for in her conversations and actions to help her guard her heart. My dad wants us all to learn how to have friends of the opposite sex so we know how to keep physical actions separate from emotional aspects in a relationship. Hopefully, we'll each only marry one person in our lifetimes, yet we'll be friends with many more. Teen years are a training ground to know how to have those friendships without physical attachments.

teen years are a training ground to know how to have friendships WITHOUT physical attachments.

My dad also wants us to have friends of the opposite sex, because he knows how important friendship is within a marriage. My dad tells us that if we want his blessing when we bring home the person we intend to marry, he'll only ask two questions: "Is he or she a follower of Jesus Christ and is he or she your best friend?"

A dad I respect told me that if a man has only two truly

"best friends" over his lifetime, he should consider himself blessed. Friendliness—the actions of being winsome, polite, respectful, positive, and courteous—is the foundation to almost every relationship that exists. My dad has helped me see that to be a friend, I need to be friendly first. Ideally, a friend and I must be equally yoked in our faith, we must both put our interests above our own, and we must give time to them and find ways to have fun. Not every relationship will involve all these traits, but how I relate to all people begins with who I am and what my character is like.

Then there are life skills.

to be a coach

you must be actively

INVOLVED in your

teen's life

I've got a friend named Brian. I love the guy, but he doesn't have a clue on how to provide for himself when he's on his own. Whenever we go out to coffee or lunch, I pay. He struggles with money management to the point it harms his social life—he tells me it's tough for him to go out on a date because he can never afford one. When a dad coaches a teen well, the teen will learn a strong work ethic and financial management skills.

Dads, without this guidance while your teens are under your roof, kids are left to figure this stuff out for themselves.

And the results aren't always pretty.

Once, shortly after getting my driver's license, I was out driving and my tire went flat. My dad had coached me in a lot of things, but he hadn't taught me yet how to change a tire. So I grabbed the jack and jumped in. Only when I let the car down and stood back to admire my work did I notice that that tire stuck out six inches more than the others. I had put the wheel on backwards!

Or take cooking. I can't tell you how many college students I know who have no idea of how to cook. I've got a good friend who lives in an apartment—check out his refrigerator and you'll find only condiments and sodas. He could use some coaching!

PRACTICAL POINTERS: A COACH'S PLAYBOOK

What does it take to coach a teen? Here are a few suggestions:

Protect the relationship first
I heard a story told by author John Trent regarding his experiences playing football. During one game his coach got so mad that he pulled John out of the game and had him sit on the bench. As John complained to the player next to him, the other guy said: "Well at least he knows your name—he doesn't even know I exist."

Dads, to be a coach you must be actively involved in your teen's life. No father would ever forget his teen's name, but it's not uncommon for kids to tell me their dads have given up on them.

Through your closeness and friendship with your teen, mutual trust and respect will develop and grow your intimacy. Your involved relationship with your teen will affect the way he or she makes choices. When trust and respect are present, freedom is granted so a teen can test his wings knowing Dad is always there to catch him if he falls.

Set clear directions and guidelines

It is important during "practice" time to provide clear directions and boundaries for behavior. Life has rules—some of which can sound unfair to a teen—but really, rules give us freedom. When we follow speed limit signs we can all drive safely on the road. When we show up for work on time, we get paid. If boundaries are violated, there are consequences. Dads who set clear boundaries with their teens tell me they simply identify what guidelines exist and why. Once the guidelines are in place, communicating expectations is the key.

For example, I had a firm curfew when I was a teen, but it was also flexible if I communicated otherwise. Say I went to a concert with some friends. My parents would know what time the concert would end, if I was going to get something to eat afterward, and what time I should reasonably be home at. We'd agree on a curfew together. My role was to get home by that time. If something came up and I was going to be out later, there was an expectation that I'd phone. My dad might agree and extend the curfew, or he might tell me I need to come home at the agreed upon time.

My dad would train me to have various life skills in the same manner. We might be doing a project around the house, for example, and he'd tell me to go to the store to get a new piece of glass for a picture frame—but that would be it. I'd have to figure out the right store, what size was needed, what type of glass to buy, and how to put the frame together. After I succeeded with smaller tasks, he'd give me larger ones, like how to find a good used car and negotiate a fair price. My dad knew I'd have to do all this stuff anyway once I moved out, so he wisely let me practice it while he was with me.

Allow your teen to fail

Dads tell me that allowing a teen to fail can be one of the toughest, but best lessons a teen will ever learn.

When I was seventeen I was involved in setting up prayer groups in public high schools across Colorado. That year I also set up a nonprofit, student-led organization that hosted youth rallies across the country. Our team of students created a board for the organization, and some very qualified businessmen were on the board.

> **allowing a teen**
> to fail can be one of the toughest, but BEST lessons a teen will ever learn

After the Columbine shootings occurred, our group got so many requests to speak to the media that we became over-whelmed—board members and all. One problem was that my confidence over-powered my lack of experience in leading a team and running a nonprofit organization. Too often I led with self-assurance and not with wise council. The result was that the team disbanded after two years. I take responsibility for that failure.

find a middle

ground between

controlling AND

coaching

But I am also so thankful I was allowed to fail. I learned incredible lessons that now guide me years later. These lessons are crucial to a similar group's work today as we set up a youth ministry that hosts evangelistic crusades across the nation.

Keep the goal of independence in mind

My dad says one of the hardest things he finds in parenting is trying to find a middle ground between controlling and coaching. He says he often wants to reel his kids in and pro-tect them from the world. He knows we need him. We all want someone in our lives who always cares for our best interests, watches over us, and loves us unconditionally—just like our heavenly Father. But just like our heavenly Father, my dad aims to not control us. He aims to guide us through his words, prayer, and counsel.

Really, my dad and I both want the same thing—we both want me to be independent. We want me to be able to handle freedom with self-discipline and responsibility. My dad says this is the secret to maintaining a close relationship while his kids learn to handle independence: Parent in such a way so as to balance kids' times of freedom with their demonstrations of responsibility.

How does this work? My senior year of high school I asked my dad if I could take a coed road trip with one other guy and three girls. (I liked the odds.) Many of my friends' parents would have been shocked if their teens had asked them if they could go. But Dad knew freedom and responsibility go hand in hand. He and I put a plan together to stay at friends and families' houses along the way. So we went. And we had a great time! Our parents trusted us and respected our judgment. In turn, our respect for our parents grew as well.

Just lean back

Our dad was a troop leader when my brother and I were in Boy Scouts. Once, we all went rock climbing together. I remember standing at the top of a forty-foot drop, all roped up and ready to descend. The guide said, "Just lean back over the rock's edge." Talk about a very unnatural thing to do! My dad told me later that he felt like that as a parent sometimes. He purposely put himself in situations where he no longer had direct control over his kids' decisions. He had to trust the rope and the skill of the guide.

Sometimes Dad refers to teens as *recycled toddlers*. He obviously knows teens are more developed than they were during the waddling years, but like toddlers, teens often want to take all a parent teaches them and try it out for themselves. A dad's role in this place is to give the freedom a teen wants, coupled with the guidance a teen needs.

How can you become the greatest coach your teen will ever know? Just lean back and look over the ledge.

DADS IN ACTION

A CHECKLIST FOR "PLEASE BE MY COACH"

- ☑ A coach guides and directs from alongside.

- ☑ Home is your teen's most important practice field.

- ☑ Coaches help players to apply what they know.

- ☑ What practical life skill can you pass on to your teen today?

- ☑ Have you been clear on what a "win" looks like?

- ☑ You may need to allow your teen to fail.

 **8**

THE SEARCH FOR THE MISSING ME

"DAD, PLEASE HELP ME FIGURE OUT WHO I AM."

I THINK IT WAS the day after my fifteenth birthday that I burned all my clothes. Yep, had a big bonfire on the front lawn and danced around in my briefs with the neighbors watching.

Well, not really, but I may as well have.

When I was younger, I dressed just like my dad—blue button-down shirts, khaki pants—just basic American stuff.

But somewhere around fifteen all that changed. All my old clothes wore out. Burned on the front lawn, as it were. I had to be me.

Who was I now? Picture Punk colliding with 1920s—the look was called "Ska." Vintage T-shirts were in, so I loaded up on them. Big, baggy suits were cool. Wearing suspenders with spiky belts and wristbands made a strange combination, but my friends and I sported them anyway. We rummaged around in thrift stores and bought old-man loafers. We painted the shoes with black and white checkerboard designs using Sharpies and White Out.

Perfect, I thought.

My dad just stared and shook his head.

What happened to me is not different from what most teenagers experience, although styles and fads can change seasonally and depend on what part of the country kids live in. I was simply feeling that age-old urge to break loose from my parents and experience life on my own. Dressing the way I wanted was a huge chunk of that. Listening to my own music played a part, too. Becoming my own person was something I never consulted my parents about first—it just happened.

For the most part, Dad overlooked my taste in clothes and music. But one night when I went out, I pushed the boundaries Dad laid out for me. The next morning we had a powwow in the living room. I remember sitting there with my jaw half open and eyes glazed over. Dad pushed and prodded to find out why I had gone against his council. It seemed my every answer was: "I dunno."

Now that I look back, I know exactly what I was doing. I don't condone conduct that smacks of disrespect like that night—but my actions then were simply part of the stage I was in. It was my way of letting Dad know I was trying to figure out who I was.

THE TEEN IN THE MIRROR

Seeking the answer to the question of identity can be the ultimate hunt for any young person. In the last six years of my travels around the U.S., this longing for identity is one of the strongest cries I hear. Teens want to know they have a purpose and place in this world. They want to know they can be the person they're becoming and still be accepted.

More than once as a teen, I've looked into my eyes in the mirror and been hard-pressed to recognize myself. So many changes happen so fast, and through them

there's a struggle to know what "real" is

all there's a struggle to know what "real" is. Teens I know tell me they stare into their mirrors, too. Sometimes the face staring back tells them good stuff, but often the face whispers lies to them. Teens are told they're ugly, stupid, or failures. Whatever is said, the biggest question teens whisper back to their reflections is: "Who are you?"

For most young people, the majority of their crucial life-decisions will be made between the ages of fifteen and twenty-five. They'll choose a college or trade, a career path, perhaps a spouse, and whether or not they will trust a Savior for eternity. They'll figure out their personality style, their strengths and limitations, their tendencies and habits. They'll probably try out different styles for a while. They may even try out different personalities—all the time trying to figure out what it means to be them.

sometimes, teens want SPACE to figure stuff out themselves

Dads, helping a teen answer these questions is not easy. Sometimes, teens want space to figure stuff out themselves. Sometimes teens need a hand making decisions. Teens tell me it's usually a bit of both. But whether from a distance or close by, teens tell me they appreciate their dads' support. As teens make these forming decisions that shape their life as well as their identity, dads can be rudders that help guide them through life's open waters. I believe the final thing teens want to say to their dads (but don't) is this: *"Dad, please help me figure out who I am."*

That huge question of identity actually hides other pressing questions:

"What should I do next?"

"How should I plan my life?"

"What core beliefs should I build my life on?"

"Do I have a future?"

Here's what I hear teens saying:

"I totally don't know where I'm going to go to college next year," said Natalie, eighteen, from California. "All I know is I want to get out of the house for a while."

"I decided to quit band this year and take art instead," said Nathaniel, fifteen, of Colorado. "My band teacher was really bummed at me, but I just don't want to spend all that energy doing something I don't want to do."

"There's these two seniors in my youth group that are really cool," said Stacey, fourteen, from Michigan "One is totally loud and outgoing, the other is sort of tough and quiet. I don't know which one of them I want to be like most."

"I took this first year after graduation off," said Robert, nineteen, from California. "I know I've got to make some money before I do anything. My parents want me to make it on my own, but it's pretty tough. I'm living in a motel and my car needs a new head gasket. I don't know how I'll ever save enough to go to school."

"I want to work at camp this summer, but my dad said I need to work at Burger King instead," said Vince, sixteen, of

Maryland. "How can I let him know that camp *is* work? I'll learn a lot of stuff there, and leading kids to Christ is totally important. That's the kind of thing I want to be involved in."

"I don't know if Alex is the right guy for me or not," said Elisa, seventeen, from Nebraska. "He's already asked me to marry him after we graduate, but I think I want to get an apartment in town with some girlfriends first."

THE GREENHOUSE AT HOME

In my dad's parenting seminars, he talks about how teens can often view themselves through the eyes of others. How teens think someone else views them can determine how they view themselves. This is where a parent must step in and ensure that teens are being encouraged to be the person God has designed them to be. A teen's character and identity are ultimately formed in Christ. Dads can be strong supporters in driving this point home. This

we are all so OVERWHELMED by the opportunities that lie before us

works on a personality level, and also for a career path. I remember talking to my dad once with some of my buddies when we were teens. The theme of our conversation was basically: *"We are all so overwhelmed by the opportunities that lie before us.*" Doesn't that just sum up so much of what teens feel—both with who they are and who they are to become?

Dads I respect say that while their teens are still under their roofs, the teens are in an ideal place for their identity to grow—a type of greenhouse, if you will. Think about what a greenhouse does—it's a safe place, protected and sheltered to some extent, yet it's also a place of purpose. Things in a greenhouse are intentionally helped to become hearty and able to withstand pressures outside the greenhouse. As a father you can help your teen find the answers to the questions of his or her identity by making the most of their time in the greenhouse. Dads say this is best accomplished by allowing teens to explore different passions for the future, develop character in the present, and understand the significance from their past.

Identity doesn't have to be a mystery! One of my dad's aims with us kids is to help us understand the hope found in Jeremiah 29:11—that God knows the plans He has for each of us. Part of the answer to our identities comes when we understand our gifts, abilities, tendencies, interests, and the paths and purposes God lays out before us. My dad helps us by collecting as many pieces of the puzzle as possible so we make wise choices. He's encouraged us to take career assessments and surveys found through our schools and spiritual gift inventories available at church. The point is to help us connect the dots between our spiritual gifts, physical talents, personalities, and career interests.

For example, my brother Jake has discovered he's a good encourager. He's also wise. So my dad has supported him in his desire to become a child psychologist. My sister Janae really likes caring for people. So my dad has encouraged her to pursue her interest in nursing. My interests are theology and speaking, so I'm at Moody Bible Institute studying to become a pastor while keeping up with my speaking. I've also noticed the assessments prompt some great conversations with Dad, as well as encouraging introspection and direction in me. Tools such as these help dads invest in a teen's future. It's part of the process of helping your teens discover who they are.

THE STRANGE PATH OF GOD'S LOVE

Dads, even though identity is not a mystery, you'll probably notice the path can be windy and foggy as your teen emerges in his or her understanding of identity. This can happen with the best guidance available. Sometimes, I envy the kids who say from the time they're three: "I'm going to be an architect when I grow up," and then take the straightest line to that place as they grow up. But it's the rare person who does that. Dads I respect say it's not uncommon to bounce around from interest to interest, place to place, even career to career, before we fully understand the strange road God's love is leading us down. So many times in life we'll go through experiences where we say: "Wow, I never planned for that"—yet it happens.

I believe there's much to be said for allowing God to write a life story for us. When we fully trust Him as a good father and know that He cares for us, it's so much easier to submit to His plan for our lives. What does it mean for God to write our life story? Does it mean we never take any initiative of our own? Not at all. But it means we pray a lot and ask for God's guidance. By His hand we can see through the fog and unexpected circumstances to a God who is behind it all.

I think there are at least three essential elements for a teen to surrender his or her identity formation to Christ:

1. Know that God is in control

When teens give their faith to Christ they are handing the pen of their lives to God. He is now authoring the story. God is a God of outcome, and He has the final product in mind. Romans 8:28 says that in all things God works for the good of those who love Him. When believing teens understand this part of their new life in Christ, they know every day has a purpose and their life's content comes from the very Creator of their souls.

How does knowing God is in control help? Think about all the things in a teen's life he or she has no control over...

- If a teen's grandparent dies, God is in control.
- If a teen's parents get divorced, God is still good.
- If a teen transfers schools in the middle of her senior year, God knows where she's going.

- If a teen becomes paralyzed from a car accident, God allowed it to happen for some reason.
- If a teen's friends are killed in a horrendous school shooting, God is still God!

2. Know that Jesus erases mistakes

I can't tell you the number of teens who tell me they think God can't love them because they've messed up. They're sure that because of some mistake in their past, God has wiped them away from His favor. So why even pray then, they say, if God thinks I'm a loser?

When teens talk to me like that I remind them sin is a fatal disease, but not incurable. We're promised freedom and life through the blood of Christ. All teens will have mistakes in the pages of their lives they wish they could erase, but the solution is not to dwell on them, or think life is ruined—the solution is confession. First John 1:9 says if we confess our sins He is faithful and just to forgive and cleanse us from all unrighteousness.

they think

GOD can't love them

because they've

MESSED up

Dads, you can help teens understand that the errors in their story are gone when they have faith in Christ and ask for His forgiveness. The only eraser marks are found at the cross—on the hands and feet of Jesus. There, our sin was erased forever.

3. Know that God holds the end of our story

Sometimes I hear from teens who have part-time jobs that they can't stand. Usually they simply need reminding that any great career will take several jobs along the way, and they may not enjoy every one of those jobs. But also, I joke with them that what they're really longing for is to be gardeners. If it weren't for Adam and Eve and their sin, we'd all still be in Eden, looking after the best plants in paradise!

Paradise is what we're created for. As believers in Christ we know that our day-to-day lives are a means to an end. We are pilgrims in this land. We are waiting to go home. An identity can be solidified when a teen's eyes are directed to see this hope. We don't live for this world, but we wait to go home and be with our Father.

YOUR POWER AS DAD

I'm twenty-three now, and I still don't know exactly who I am or what I'll be doing in life. But my identity is secure. My destiny is in Christ, and He does not fail. My dad has been my biggest cheerleader over the past several years in helping me learn that. He's helped me sift through what I've thought about myself, or what I've imagined others are saying about me. Best of all, he's helped me understand the truth of what God thinks about me.

Dads, I know you can do the same for your teen. Be with them when they ask questions and when they're silent. Help them think through all they can become and hope to be. Help them quiet the lies and shout the truths about themselves. Because no matter what confusion they feel now, they were put on this earth for a good and important reason—and in Christ, they *do* have an amazing future.

DADS IN ACTION

A CHECKLIST FOR "HELP ME FIGURE OUT WHO I AM."

- [x] Most teens try on identities like clothes.
  (Try not to panic!)

- [x] Good dads help teens connect the dots
  (between their abilities, passions, personalities, and
  opportunities).

- [x] Mistakes aren't the end of a story.

- [x] God is in control—and He is good!

EPILOGUE:

A FATHER'S GREATEST GIFT

LET'S TAKE AWAY everything else for a moment, and just let me share what is strongest on my heart.

If I could say anything to you at all, it would be this—*Dads, please show your teen the way to God.* By far the biggest impact on my spiritual life has been my dad's open demonstration of living his values and beliefs in front of me. I know very clearly that my dad loves the Lord. He follows Jesus Christ with all his heart. He desires to serve God and walk in His paths. I can't tell you what an impact that has on me now and has had on me while growing up!

Teens tell me over and over again, when it comes to their faith, they want to see their dads living for the Lord. Some dads call themselves believers but hardly talk about their faith—its trials and triumphs—or demonstrate their love and commitment for God apart from going to church. Other dads are quick to drop off their teens at youth activities or to put up money to send them to camp, but are incapable of modeling what a personal relationship with Christ looks like in their own lives.

Other dads I know are succeeding in this area. They may talk about their struggle with the silence of God as well as their strength coming from God out of their quiet times in God's Word and prayer. They ask their teens what they are going though spiritually, or about a struggle or a decision they have, or about what God is telling them. These are the dads who ask their teens questions like: Have you spent time in prayer? Where in the Bible are you reading right now? How are you growing in your relationship with Christ? These are the dads who pray for their teens with passion and fervency. These are the dads who know they need Christ in their lives like they need their next breath.

teens want to

see their dads living

for the LORD

A FATHER'S GREATEST GIFT

Once my dad asked me to attend a speaking engagement with him. He wanted me to answer the question; "Why do teens *not* accept Christ?" I identified three reasons that came from conversations with teens. First, dads need to show that God is real. Second, dads need to show that God is relevant. Third, dads need to say and do the same thing—they can't be hypocritical in their faith.

My dad followed up my talk that day by encouraging the men in that room to be models of the love and grace of Christ for their teens. "A dad's life should so reflect his commitment to the Lord that his teens will want the same thing in their lives," he said. Too many men relegate their faith to Sunday mornings only. Yet teens should not see any difference between Sunday morning and the rest of the week. Dads—please, be men of integrity. The two greatest commands are to love the Lord your God with all your heart, mind, and soul and to love your neighbor as yourself. God should be our purpose and our passion. Our lives need to reflect that.

Your teens love you and want you in their lives. They want you to show them all that is good and holy and right and pure. They want your presence, your encouragement, your time, and your love. All this is within your power to give. And the best thing of all you could ever do for them is help them find the way to God.

There is no greater gift a father can give.

I'm thankful for what you're doing today to invest in your children and in the next generation. And I'm confident that, with God's grace and power, even greater things are ahead for you and your teen.

God bless you!

—*Josh*

THank you...

Bill Savier for endlessly supporting me.

Verna Pauls for warmly housing me.

David Kopp for gently mentoring me.

Marcus Brotherton for so eloquently speaking for me.

Don Jacobson for believing in me.

Doug Gabbert for patiently pursuing me.

My family for incessantly encouraging me.

Molly, Maureen, and Jim for loving and praying for me.

Elmbrook Church for listening to me.

The Multnomah staff for passionately partnering with me.

This message would have never gotten out without all of your help, thank you!

TO LEARN MORE ABOUT **JOSH WEIDMANN**

Find him on the Internet at:

www.joshweidmann.info

www.multnomah.net/weidmann

Find out more about Josh and how
his messages are changing the lives of
young people everywhere.

LEARN MORE ABOUT **JIM WEIDMANN**
AND HIS MINISTRY

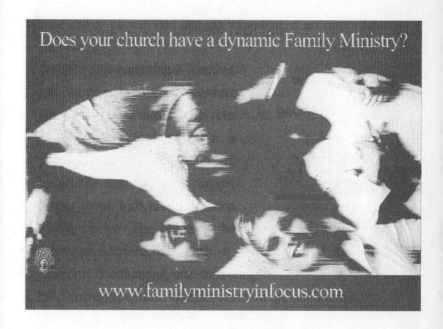

Does your church have a dynamic Family Ministry?

www.familyministryinfocus.com

Find him on the Internet at:

www.familyministryinfocus.com

YOUR TEEN, YOUR LEGACY

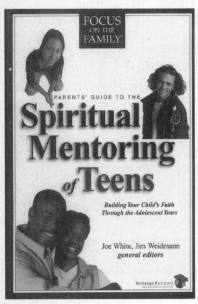

1-56179-891-6

Parents' Guide to the Spiritual Mentoring of Teens
WITH JIM WEIDMANN

The teen years are critical to developing adult children who know, love, and serve the Lord. This guide offers solid, proven advice and techniques that will enable you to succeed in the changing parent-teen relationship. It will also equip you to ignite a passion in your teens to become wholehearted disciples.